MOTOWN

&
the Arrival
of
Black Music

DAVID MORSE

Studio Vista

Produced by November Books Limited,
23–29 Emerald Street, London WC1N
3QL.

Published by Studio Vista Limited,
Blue Star House, Highgate Hill,
London N19.

Typeset, printed and bound by The
Tinling Printing Group, Warrington
Road, Prescot, Lancashire, L34 2TJ.

© November Books Limited 1971.

Printed in England.

This edition is not for sale in the United
States of America.

Edited by Phil Hardy

Dust-jacket and paperback cover designed by David Goard.

Designed by Tom Carter.
House editor: Tony Russell.
Copy preparation: John Leath.

SBN 289.70131.7 (hardback)
     289.70130.9 (paperback)

ACKNOWLEDGEMENTS

I should like to thank the following for
their assistance: Bill Millar for photographic research, Geoff Altman for the
loan of many valuable records, and
Norman Duval of EMI for his help with
both photographic and recorded material.
I am also very grateful to the Carlin
Music Corporation for permission to
quote from lyrics in their copyright.

Contents

Introduction

Motown has been in existence for only a decade, but in that relatively brief time it has become one of the dominant forces in popular music. It has stamped its mark indelibly on the '60s; has survived, as is always necessary, many changes in fashion; and at the beginning of the '70s is firmly at the centre of the music scene. It is practically an institution. Yet Motown is a black company, which until recently has featured black artists almost exclusively; and it has been built up by Berry Gordy and his associates from practically nothing, to become one of the most successful businesses in America. But there is more to this story than business or musical expertise. Motown today is part of a whole series of complex changes in the shape and structure of popular music since the beginnings of rock 'n' roll. It is easy to think of Motown as constituting a distinct musical category; it has an identifiable sound, comes from Detroit, and in Britain is issued on the Tamla Motown label. Admittedly there are times when Motown seems like an island in the middle of popular music, shaken and buffetted by the raging seas of hard rock and soul music, deluged by strings and schmaltz, yet somehow hanging on to its own chart-orientated identity. To understand what the Motown phenomenon represents it is necessary to set it in a wider musical and cultural context; to show where it came from and what it led to, how it was influenced by other music, how it exercised an influence of its own, and how it was itself modified and altered by later trends.

To look back over the history of 20th-century popular music is both disquieting and exhilarating. Disquieting, because time and time again the vital music of black America, whether ragtime or gospel, traditional or modern jazz, country or urban blues, has been plundered, stolen, adapted, modified, cleaned-up and diluted out of existence. Even today one cannot be confident that this destructive cycle has finally been broken. Exhilarating, because this music has proved so strong that it has kept on coming back, not merely surviving but constantly renewing itself. Thus today jazz is played in the Soviet Union and rock has become an unstoppable world-wide phenomenon, undermining the traditional commercial music of countries as different as France, Italy, Germany and Japan. Those comical teenagers who, in 1956, said that rock 'n' roll was here to stay have been proved right, though at the time it appeared as disruptive and impractical as a steam-driven automobile.

Rock 'n' roll arrived at a moment when the emasculation of the jazz heritage was virtually complete; when the complex polyphony of New Orleans jazz at its best had been transformed into the tastefully variegated musical wallpaper of Glenn Miller and his descendants, for whom solo improvisation had become no more than a device for lightening the orchestral texture. It came when dance-band and cinema receipts were falling as the over-30s stayed at home watching television. The vacuum they left, in music and the movies, was filled by a new youth culture.

Rock 'n' roll was never a coherent musical movement. From start to finish it was a chapter of accidents, a shaky powder trail that just happened to set off a keg of dynamite. No one really knew what rock 'n' roll was except that it was music with a beat which was played on Alan Freed's radio show 'Rock 'n' Roll Party'. Freed was a classical DJ who had heard and dug the music of Buddy Johnson and other rhythm-and-blues bands and had asked for a spot in which to feature them. But in the early days the concept was rather vague, and a few months passed before the radio men found out that Count Basie was playing the wrong beat and dropped him from the show. There was a demand for rock 'n' roll before there was anything to fill the bill, and the rock 'n' roll stars were a strange collection of misfits from country-and-western and rhythm-and-blues, summoned into existence by an eager public and welded into cohesion by the hot breath of the excited mass media.

What Bill Haley offered was essentially a modified hoedown, at which he presided as a kind of master-of-ceremonies. What became identified as rock 'n' roll consisted largely of novelty vocal routines ('One o'clock, two o'clock, three o'clock rock'; 'See you later, alligator'), the steady thud of a bass, throbbing triplet figures punctuated by a crashing afterbeat and a honking tenor saxophone solo in which the musician thrust his horn in the air and lay back as if attempting to touch the floor with the back of his head. The connection with the rhythm-and-blues of such figures as Joe Turner, Chuck Berry or Elmore James was tenuous, to say the least, even if Haley had his first big hit with an emasculated version of Turner's *Shake, Rattle And Roll*. Such associations as there were in rhythm-and-blues lay in the 'novelty' music of the jump bands, led by Earl Bostic, Amos Milburn, Roy Brown, Wynonie Harris and, above all, Louis Jordan, who appears to have prompted Haley's line in bastardised jive talk. But it is very doubtful whether Haley on his own could have created the movement called rock 'n' roll. For him the backbeat was simply a musical sauce which could be added to any familiar recipe. (One of his first hits was *Mambo Rock*, at a time when there was also a Mambo craze, and this hybrid was answered by another in Kay Starr's *Rock And Roll Waltz*. *The Saints Rock And Roll* followed.) Two factors helped to change the situation: religious opposition in the South and Elvis Presley.

Bill Haley's music had already become associated with teenage rebellion, because it had been used by Richard Brooks in his film *Blackboard Jungle* (1955), but it was religious opposition that turned rock 'n' roll into a controversial, newsworthy issue. In May 1956, in Birmingham, Alabama, worthy citizens paraded with placards which carried such messages as 'Ask your preacher about jungle music'. Not for the first or the last time, white 'civilisation' was seen as being on trial. Southerners clearly perceived the lurid threat of the Negro and suspected, probably correctly, that in rock 'n' roll there was something a little subversive. In the mid-'50s American society was as submissive and acquiescent as at almost any period in its history. In the wake of Senator Joseph McCarthy there were still tremendous pressures to conform, and the cold war psychosis ruled. Menaces were seen everywhere. So we should not be very surprised that the White Citizens' Council linked rock 'n' roll with sin, degradation and communism, even though in the Soviet Union, at the same time, it was taken as epitomising Western decadence. In those repressed and anxious times rock 'n' roll was the first little puff of steam to tilt the lid of the kettle.

Rock 'n' roll did offer certain distinct financial advantages – it promised to fill the dance halls again and at a lower cost, because a seven-piece rock band was substantially cheaper than a full dance-orchestra. But it is doubtful whether it would ever have made an impact without Elvis Presley. Where Elvis found his unique style has been a matter of much inconclusive debate. He has been compared to, to name but a few, Little Junior Parker and Arthur 'Big Boy' Crudup, whose numbers he recorded when he was with Sun Records; with Johnny Ray and Billy Daniels; even with Bill Kenny, the lead singer of The Inkspots; but in fact he does not sound like any of them. It is probable that the blues influences on Presley have been exaggerated, but there can be no doubt that he had listened to a good deal of relatively unknown black music – like his predecessor as a teenage idol, Johnny Ray, who in an interview confessed to an interest in 'a whole heap of blues singers, whose work does not seem to be widely known in Britain, such as Ruth Brown, 'Miss Share-cropper', Dinah Washington, 'Miss Cornshucks' and James Rushing'. Such music probably encouraged Presley, as it did Ray, to sing in a more emotional, exclamatory style. The sombre, closed style of delivery which he adopts on his early discs is definitely blues-influenced; but his fondness for jagged, angular rhythms, which he shares with Carl Perkins and Jerry Lee Lewis, clearly places him in the country-and-western tradition and makes 'rockabilly' the most appropriate description for white rock 'n' roll.

The early rock records became symbolic of the inarticulate rebellion of a new generation. One was either fascinated or repelled by echo-chambered gasps, grunts and mumbles. Reviewing *Heartbreak Hotel* in the *Melody Maker* Laurie Henshaw commented that 'Presley's diction – or the original recording balance – is extremely poor', while Steve Race wrote: 'for sheer repulsiveness, coupled with the monotony of incoherence *Hound Dog* hit a new low in my experience,' and 'Harlequin', reviewing a Gene Vincent disc in *The Gramophone*, protested, 'I know exactly what is meant by the living end, except that he sounds like a Dead-End Kid, gurgling and juddering incoherently'. Jack Payne demanded 'Should We Surrender to the Teenagers?' For Steve Race the acclaim for Presley meant the end of any conceivable criteria – good voice, good tune, and so forth – for judging popular music, although he still expressed his faith in 'the masses who still want to hear a tuneful song, tunefully sung.' But the prospects seemed dire, and, had anyone thought of it at the time, they might well have spoken of the impending downfall of Western European humanism.

The success of rock, however, was by no means the triumph it has sometimes been pictured, least of all in Britain. In the United States, for example, Doris Day's *Whatever Will Be, Will Be*, from Hitchcock's remake of *The Man Who Knew Too Much* (1956), was shut out from the Number 1 spot by Elvis's *Hound Dog* and the Platters' *My Prayer*, but in Britain it zoomed effortlessly to the top, with good old-fashioned fare in the form of Anne Shelton's *Lay Down Your Arms* and Teresa Brewer's *Sweet Old-fashioned Girl* close behind. Rock 'n' roll nevertheless brought about some striking changes. *Melody Maker*, which had previously listed only best-selling sheet music, followed the *New Musical Express* in listing the top records. Moreover, the making of cover versions, which for years had provided British singers with their bread and butter as they vainly endeavoured to compete with Mitch Miller's CBS stable of Guy Mitchell, Johnny Ray, Rosemary Clooney, Doris Day and Frankie Laine, gradually went into a decline. In April 1956 *Melody Maker* listed as many as eight cover versions of *It's Almost Tomorrow* and *Memories Are Made of This*, but for *Heartbreak Hotel*, hardly surprisingly, there was no cover version at all. It was the birth of the new Hit Record – unique and, sometimes even for the artist, unrepeatable.

In the rock 'n' roll era black music still travelled in the rear seat; black artists were called in, like hired hands, only because there

10

A Motown advertisement from Billboard, *March 1967.*

were not enough white musicians to do the job. Anyway, there was little in common between the pounding, lugubrious rhythm-and-blues of Fats Domino, the intense, quasi-religious ballad styling of The Platters and the intricate, incomprehensible, gospel-influenced hollering of Little Richard. Little Richard stole the show in every rock 'n' roll movie in which he appeared – but only as an electrifying curiosity. Between him and his white audience there lay an un-bridgeable gulf, and Little Richard was shouting from across the far side.

The basic problem of rock 'n' roll was that although it was music *for* teenagers it was not the music *of* teenagers. They could respond to the sound, but hardly identify with the musicians; the black artists were strange, alien and usually too old, while Bill Haley, despite the kisscurl, was no one's idea of a dream lover. While at the later public performances of The Beatles and at some open-air concerts there was a kind of participation, rock 'n' roll preserved a sense of distance. Perhaps this was why it was transferred so easily to the movies, where the spectator could simultaneously be in-volved in the music and watch with detached fascination.

The gap between performer and spectator was bridged by High School music. High School music was a manufactured product founded on the fine old principle that freedom is the right to supply people with what they want at a percentage. Stars were created: Fabian, Frankie Avalon, Tommy Sands and many, depressingly many more. Song titles began to reflect teenage experiences: *At The Hop, Stood Up, Waitin' In School, Puppy Love, Breakin' Up Is Hard To Do, Problems*. They used teenage slang (as in Neil Sedaka's *I Go Ape*) and emphasised humiliating experiences – *Someone's Fool*, The Everlys' *Bird Dog* and *Cathy's Clown*. Other songs described sentimental love, going steady and so forth. There was Bobby Vinton's *Roses Are Red*, and there were Paul and Paula, who appeared on the cover of their LP 'We Go Together' in blazers bearing a large red P, coyly sharing a soda-fountain speciality. It was something of a disappointment when they announced to their fans 'We are going to get married – but not to each other.'

High School music was the froth on a daydream, but elsewhere fundamental changes were taking place. Rock 'n' roll had shown country-and-western and rhythm-and-blues that there was a way out of their ghetto market and specialised audiences. Not sur-prisingly it was the milder, whiter, more sentimental country music that benefited most, although R & B was able to haul itself up a little on country-music coat-tails. Rock 'n' roll itself died almost before it had begun. Haley's hits trailed away as their novelty value wore off and on a later LP, 'I Dig Chicks', he even eliminated the trademarked backbeat. Little Richard went back into the church.

Elvis was inducted into the army, and from a symbol of rebellion was transformed into a model soldier. With *It's Now Or Never* and *Are You Lonesome Tonight?* he showed that it was possible to retain a brooding erotic appeal, while dispensing with the shake and the rattle. Rock 'n' roll's last gasp was in the huge hits by The Coasters and Lloyd Price, *Yakety Yak*, *Charlie Brown*, and *Stagger Lee*, which proved that R & B could talk High School language. Otherwise, it was a time of guitars and country music, as others rushed to acquire Elvis's Nashville expertise. Carl Perkins and Jerry Lee Lewis returned to their country-music roots. Country-and-western stars like Marvin Rainwater, Johnny Cash, Marty Robbins, Jim Reeves, The Everly Brothers, Bobby Bare, Leroy Van Dyke, and John D. Loudermilk, and guitarists like Chet Atkins, Duane Eddy and Hank Garland, acquired a wide following and became the mainstays of popular music. In a still more commercial vein was the Elvis-influenced but definitely country-tinged delivery of Roy Orbison. Orbison's material, like Elvis's, emphasised loneliness and melancholy and he produced albums with such titles as 'Lonely and Blue', 'Only the Lonely', and 'Cryin''. Del Shannon sang Hank Williams numbers and, although not strictly a C & W singer, drew from a maudlin repertoire that clearly had its roots there, in such songs as *Cry Myself To Sleep, I Wake Up Crying* and *Stains On My Letter*; while in one of his best-known hits he pantingly warned his listeners of possible pain in store – you could get 'hu-hu-hu-hu-hurt' by that little flirt. It was a weepy age.

The years from 1958 to 1962 were a period of doldrums in popular music, marked by the death of all that was rock in rock 'n' roll. The beat was subdued by cumbersome arrangements, and Tin Pan Alley-orientated 'production values' were increasingly emphasised. For evidence of the damage that could be done it is only necessary to compare some recent records of The Supremes and Marvin Gaye with their 'We Remember Sam Cooke' and 'A Tribute to The Late Nat King Cole' LPs, which – though later recordings – were performed in the style of the period, much as though the artists had donned musical periwigs.

Technology was more significant than the music. Amplification enabled a small group to make more noise than a large orchestra. In March 1958 Keith Goodwin, reviewing a Buddy Holly concert for the *New Musical Express*, headlined it 'Holly-Crickets give us the loudest rock show yet' and noted that 'they completely overpowered the 13-piece Ronnie Keene Orchestra'. Records were similarly affected by technical developments; the achievement of a distinctive sound became more and more important, because in a period of unstable consumer loyalties it could be the x factor which changed failure to success. Stars were no longer essential; what mattered was catching the listener's attention and holding it for a vital two or three minutes. Producers left behind the world of the single microphone and became immersed in the mysteries of multi-track mixing, echo effects, overdubbing and added resonances. Recording became an end in itself. It is possible that the spread of 'Hi Fi' jukeboxes in both Britain and the United States may have done something to influence taste, since they tended drastically to over emphasise both ends of the musical spectrum; the treble projected the high, nasal intonation of Holly and the Everlys, while the enormous bass reflex chambers produced a throbbing, vibrant accompaniment. The culmination of all these developments was the work of Phil Spector. Sole author of all his productions, he treated songs, artists, instrumentation and arrangements simply as components to be assembled. Recording a single side could take as long as three days, while Spector shuffled the pieces until he felt he had discovered the right combination. He stressed sound because it was the one thing that could be constant: 'I felt it had to be dynamic enough to overcome any bad material so people would respond to the sound rather than to the song.' Spector was an innovator in his preference for a large and complex rhythm section. He would use four pianos, three guitars, three basses (two of them electric) and two drummers. All of his records have this hi-lo effect; the high voices of girl vocal groups soar above a steady, relentlessly rolling and texturally thick accompaniment. Spector also emphasised variations of tempo and texture within a song; rather as an advertising commercial tries to extend itself by switching from rapid cutting, with uptempo music, to a fireside and cellos.

Unwittingly Spector prepared the way for the upheavals that were to bury him, British rock and Motown. In retrospect his innovations appear only as preparations for the decisive shift in British and American popular music in 1963 and, perhaps more crucially, in 1964. Some of these changes were important, others relatively trivial, but all played their part in establishing Motown and all are therefore of some significance.

For example, the early period of rock had been largely dominated by male artists, but in the early '60s girl singers again began to come to the fore – first Connie Francis and Brenda Lee, then all-girl groups like The Shirelles, The Ronettes and The Crystals. Undoubtedly this trend opened a door for Motown's girl groups, Martha and The Vandellas, The Supremes, The Marvelettes and The Velvelettes. There was also a leaning towards a lighter, firmer beat, in reaction against both over-loaded swing-type arrangements and the ponderousness of rock 'n' roll at its worst. This was exemplified by Dionne Warwick's versions of songs by Burt

Bacharach, the popularity of which certainly helped to make Motown more widely acceptable outside the R & B market. The same was true of the Twist, which made rock respectable among the middle-aged middle class, providentially put a number of old-time rockers back in business, and, perhaps most important of all, produced some of the classic records of the new music, like The Isley Brothers' *Twist And Shout* and The Contours' *Do You Love Me?*, which were the springboard from which the Liverpool Sound took off.

Rudolph, Ronald and O'Kelly Isley made their best records long before joining Motown, particularly Shout *parts 1 and 2 (Victor 0589) in 1959, and* Twist And Shout *(Wand 124) in 1962.*

Though there was much plagiarism of American originals, Britain played an important role in changing the face of popular music. British trends, from skiffle to trad, from R & B to Liverpool, did to an astonishing degree represent a genuinely popular music, which emerged spontaneously from below and was manipulated, as the recording industry desperately tried to tag along, without suffering much damage. Suddenly the male rock group with guitars supplanted all other combinations. The unexpectedness of this about-turn, which followed The Beatles' *Love Me Do* and *Please Please Me*, is demonstrated by the fact that as late as September 1962 Derek Johnson could ask, in the *New Musical Express*, 'What's Happened to the Vocal Groups?' and point to their total absence from the charts. The success of The Beatles and other British groups helped Motown in at least three ways. In the first place, the emphasis on groups helped black music, in which they had always been important, and Motown in particular. In the wake of The Beatles' publicity it became natural for the *New Musical Express* to run a feature 'A Four Top A Week' and for The Supremes to issue an album signed by Mary, Florence and Diana. Secondly, and more arguably, the raucous, uninhibited style of early British rock encouraged interest in the models. Chuck Berry began to appear regularly in the British charts. Two versions of *Twist And Shout* (by Brian Poole and The Beatles) and two of *Do You Love Me?* (by Brian Poole and The Dave Clark Five) reached the Top Ten. Only a year before the reviewer of a Contours LP had written in some perplexity: 'If you like weirdie vocal group sounds this disc is for you. This five-singers, one-guitarist group produces some wild, shouting vocals, with a different sound or two instrumentally as well. In this way, it's exciting but not everyone's meat.' In 1962 The Contours were decidedly a minority taste, but it was another story in 1963, when the Brian Poole cover evoked this comment: '*Do You Love Me* has the right sound to be a seller. It's raucous and a strain on the vocal chords, but it's bursting with excitement'.

A third and more significant factor in Motown's favour was the advocacy of The Beatles; for in 1964, in the old phrase, their favourites were everybody's favourites. The *New Musical Express* led a story on the first Motown tour of Britain, which brought over Stevie Wonder, Mary Wells, Martha and The Vandellas, The Miracles and The Contours, by saying 'The Beatles favourite artists are coming to Britain', while, in an interview in the same issue, John Lennon referred to Marvin Gaye's *Can I Get A Witness?* as one of his favourite songs. On their LP 'With The Beatles' the group recorded three Motown numbers, The Miracles' *You Really Got A Hold On Me*, Barrett Strong's *Money*, and The Marvelettes' *Please, Mr. Postman*, less as cover versions than as

The 1965 British tour played to packed houses in London, but overall was a financial disaster.

gestures of affection and admiration. In fact British groups could not hope to rival overnight the vocal interplay of the best Motown acts; their style was always more spontaneous and less disciplined.

The 'radio sound', which has been ascribed to Motown by Phil Spector and Jon Landau, raises questions of some interest. There is an intriguing parallelism between the rise of Motown and the tremendous expansion in the market for small transistor radios in the '60s. Spector's own records had too much reverberation for them to be really effective in this medium. Moreover, Motown's light, unfussy, evenly stressed beat, its continuous loop melodies, were the ideal accompaniment for driving. But the kind of musical attention involved in listening to radio, less focused than at a live concert, is more significant. In fact, it is characteristic of much contemporary music that there is no need for the listener to 'follow'. Instead of concentrating on the development of a linear progression he immerses himself in an all-embracing polyphonic immediacy that seeks to cancel time. There is an emphasis on synchronic rather than diachronic complexity. This need, if need it is, has certainly been answered by Motown, which, in its gospel origins, represents the second irruption of black polyphony in popular music–the first being New Orleans jazz, which was rapidly diluted into Dixieland and swing. But while New Orleans jazz used vocal effects – blue notes, slurs, and so on – in instrumental music, Motown, and soul music in general, employs the purely vocal styles of gospel singing. Early Motown hits like The Miracles' *Shop Around*, The Marvelettes' *Please, Mr. Postman*, The Supremes' *Where Did Our Love Go* and Martha and The Vandellas' *Heatwave* are notable for the sparseness of their instrumental texture. Voices, percussion and handclapping are brought into a direct relationship, increasingly emphasised by the hollowness of the sound. It is a return to the fundamental elements of music.

Today 'soul' is a word that is used more or less synonymously with rhythm-and-blues – the result of an extended period of change and interaction in black music. Until quite recently 'soul' was often used specifically to designate gospel-influenced music and tendencies that were antithetical to traditional R & B. The fusion of blues and gospel today is simply part of a larger process of fusion within popular music, which has seen the virtual elimination of swing and the coalescence of various forms of traditional minority music – folk, C & W, R & B and gospel – creating a musical territory almost without frontiers. The figures who have played the greatest part in shaping contemporary popular music – The Beatles, Bob Dylan, Ray Charles – have been eclectics, playing and singing in various styles yet retaining their own individuality. Dylan shook his traditional admirers by recording and playing with a rock band; later he cut a record in Nashville. Ray Charles aroused equal, if not greater indignation with his gospel-influenced rhythm-and-blues. In the black community a strict line had always been drawn between religious music and the secular blues, with their down-to-earth content and frank sexuality. Big Bill Broonzy had the choice of being either a blues singer or a preacher and he always kept the two roles quite distinct in his mind. On Ray Charles he commented: 'He's got the blues, he's cryin' sanctified. He's mixin' the blues with the spirituals. I know that's wrong.' These views were echoed by Charles's British reviewers. Charles Fox pointed out that he had altered the words of the gospel song, *When I'm Lonely I Talk To Jesus* to *I Got A Woman Way Over Town,* and strongly objected to the transformation: 'songs of passion have been changed to songs of emotion, an aesthetic blunder and a process I find cheap and embarrassing'. Alexis Korner found the result 'vaguely horrifying' and felt that there was nothing to be gained by combining the two: 'I love blues and gospel singing as individual forms, with individual functions and techniques.' It is also relevant that talk of 'soul' was once associated mainly with ballad singers, and that Sam Cooke's original reluctance to sing rock may have been due to his feeling that it was not entirely respectable.

Ray Charles then confused matters still more by recording two enormously successful albums of country-and-western music, in which he invested the banal and sentimental lyrics with genuine feeling – as, for example, in *You Don't Know Me* – and at the same time gave them a touch of shrewd blues knowingness. He thus created a beachhead from which other R & B artists were able to

An early Tamla Motown advertisement. 11 December 1961.

break out – as Solomon Burke did with the C & W song *Just Out Of Reach*.

After Ray Charles's momentous appearance at Newport in 1958, gospel motifs began to appear regularly in modern jazz. Eight- and sixteen-bar themes came to be used, as did time signatures of 3/4 and 6/8, which had hitherto been regarded as difficult, requiring a different style of drumming. On Julian Adderley's LP 'Cannonball Takes Charge' the rocking, hand-clapping, churchlike beat of Albert Heath on *Barefoot Sunday Blues* was markedly different from the flowing, driving style of Jimmy Cobb, from the Miles Davis Quintet, who was used on other tracks.

A further consequence of the Ray Charles revolution was the transformation of gospel numbers into potential hit parade material. An outstanding example of this trend was *I Found A Love* by The Falcons, a Detroit group, whose lead singer was Wilson Pickett. The totally uninhibited gospel character of this record makes most other R & B performances sound, even today, comparatively flat. The call-and-response pattern created between Pickett and the group makes for a sense of drama that is both satisfying and triumphant and in no way disproportionate to its subject. Another record strongly influenced in both style and content by gospel music was The Miracles' *Way Over There*, with hand-clapping on 'They tell me the river's too deep' and falsetto singing on 'I'm goin' away'. These discs have a fervour that has seldom been equalled since.

Gospel was the basis of the Motown style; it provided the gospel beat, the hand-clapping and tambourines, and the relationship between voices. Motown was essentially a bridge between gospel and popular music which virtually by-passed traditional rhythm and blues. Nevertheless, it has influenced the world of R & B and in turn been influenced, so that in soul music most of the old distinctions have been obliterated. Today, despite some continuing resistance, black music enjoys a world-wide popularity that would have been inconceivable only fifteen years ago, when Ray Charles recorded *Hallelujah, I Love Her So*. It no longer tags along like a poor relation, as it did in the days of rock 'n' roll; it is here in its own right. Rock 'n' roll was not the revolution; the real revolution is now.

Motown Music

It has become almost impossible to talk about Motown without referring to the Detroit or Motown 'sound'. Yet the term is extremely dated and goes back to the days when it was customary to compare the New York sound of Phil Spector with its rival in the Motor City. The phrase conjured up visions of hyper-ingenious individuals seated at master consoles, adjusting the volume level of sixteen or more different channels to find the precise combination that would draw the teenage record buyer. This fantasy appealed as much to Spector as it did to the self-appointed representatives of élite culture, who wished to present him as a sinister manipulator of juvenile masses, but it is doubtful whether it ever had much relevance to Motown, which was always something more than a particular EQ. In popular music temporary successes can be attributed to relatively trivial causes, but Motown's commanding position, after ten years' existence, as the largest seller of singles in the United States cannot be attributed to any single factor.

The music business keeps its nose to the charts, week after week, year after year. Obsessed with short-term trends, it is chronically incapable of seeing a long-term one or of responding in anything but an *ad hoc* fashion to fundamental changes in taste. When it seems impossible to assign specific reasons for the success or failure of a disc or an artist, magical attitudes prevail. It is always satisfying to believe that there is at least one A & R man, DJ or manager who possesses an infallible sense of what will be a hit and what will not, who knows the tastes of the public before it does itself. Talking about a particular 'sound' is like talking about the miracle ingredient x which soap powders are alleged to contain. What matters is not whether they have it but whether they are believed to have it. It may be that recording techniques give added presence; that a certain drummer, bass-player or guitarist can make a significant contribution to a record; or even that it is possible to achieve a more soulful sound in one recording studio than in another; but the vast significance attached to these issues is probably no more than a contemporary voodoo. There is a pathetic side to Spector's statement that Bob Dylan has never really been 'produced' – because he has to admit that Dylan doesn't need it. There is something more than production, something called music; and Motown is a whole music and not just a sound.

Before forming Tamla in 1960 Berry Gordy Jr wrote material for Jackie Wilson, and leased productions of Marv Johnson and of The Miracles to other companies.

22

Nevertheless Motown did not acquire its distinctive identity overnight. In fact it seems ironic that when Berry Gordy started out in 1959 he wanted to name his company 'Tammie', after the Debbie Reynolds hit song of the year – a number which is about as far from Motown's current image as you could possibly get. But the name had been copyrighted and he called the label Tamla instead. It was a confusing period to get into the record business. Ballads and beat numbers did equally well, and there was a succession of dance crazes. It was far from clear what people wanted, though there were plenty of promoters who were prepared to tell them. Several rhythmic styles were current; rock 'n' roll triplets lived on, but there were types of 4/4 swing drumming, there were Latin figures and embellishments, there was a special drum style for the Twist, and so on. Early Motown records do not show a clear pattern, but have a little of everything. Thus, The Miracles' *Mama Done Told Me* and *I Love You Baby* are basically rock 'n' roll numbers; *Bad Girl* and *All I Want Is You* are ballads with a triplet feel, in the style popularised by Dinah Washington; *Way Over There* is unmistakably gospel. Barrett Strong's *Money* and The Contours' *Do You Love Me?* are twist numbers. The Marvelettes' *You're My Remedy* is distinctively reminiscent of Elvis's *Good Luck Charm*. Martha and the Vandellas' *There He Is* is a Latin number, while *Tears On My Pillow* is a ballad with a rock 'n' roll beat. The Miracles' *A Love She Can Count On* is an interesting hybrid of rock 'n' roll triplets and gospel hand-clapping. And it is as well to remember, whenever it is suggested that Motown is falling away from its original high standards, that The Supremes' *A Breathtaking Guy* –

Tamla releases from The Marvelettes and Barrett Strong, as well known for his songwriting as his singing.

the disc that first brought them some recognition – was more conspicuously a piece of commercial kitsch than almost anything they have recorded since.

But Motown was undoubtedly making progress. In 1961 The Miracles' *Shop Around* went to No. 2 in the American charts and at the end of the year The Marvelettes' *Please Mr. Postman* became the first Detroit record to reach No. 1. In 1962 The Contours' *Do You Love Me?* went to No. 3, The Miracles' *Mickey's Monkey* and *You Really Got A Hold On Me* both reached No. 8, while Martha and The Vandellas' *Heat Wave* made No. 4. Stevie Wonder's *Fingertips* became another No. 1.

In Britain Motown suffered from cover versions and lacked exposure. Finally, in 1964, Mary Wells's *My Guy* reached No. 5. But it was The Supremes who were really successful, first with *Where Did Our Love Go* (No. 2) and then with *Baby Love*, which was only the second American disc to reach No. 1 in two years (the other being Roy Orbison's *It's Over*), such was the impact of Liverpool after years of American domination of the charts. In March 1965 the Tamla Motown label was launched (previous releases having been on Fontana, Oriole and Stateside) to coincide with the first Motown tour of Britain, but this was not a great success. The Supremes' *Stop In The Name Of Love* was the only Motown disc to make the Top Twenty in 1965, and in an interview Diana Ross commented, 'You just can't tell – in the States Tamla is big, over here it's nothing'. The situation was quite different in 1966; first Stevie Wonder's *Uptight* reached No. 14, then The Four Tops' *Reach Out I'll Be There* went to the top of the chart – apparently throwing the door wide open, for Motown records have consistently reached the Top Thirty since then.

It was in 1963, the year when The Beatles changed the face of British pop music, that the characteristic Motown style emerged fully formed with records like Martha and The Vandellas' *Come And Get These Memories*, Marvin Gaye's *Can I Get A Witness?*, The Miracles' *Mickey's Monkey* and *I Gotta Dance To Keep From Crying*, and The Marvelettes' *As Long As I Know He's Mine*. The Stateside EP 'R & B Chartmakers No. 2' reveals the contrast between old Motown and new, the tracks by The Miracles and The Marvelettes (mentioned above) making Kim Weston's *Love Me All The Way* and The Supremes' *A Breathtaking Guy* seem productions of an altogether different era. But by 1964 both The Supremes and Kim Weston had boarded the train, with *Where Did Our Love Go?* and *Looking For The Right Guy* respectively. It is easy to see what linked these records – they were gospel-influenced popular music, and the train was a gospel train.

Gospel music was becoming increasingly popular, partly

because of Ray Charles, but also because of an increased interest in all forms of traditional music – a result of the boom in 'folk'. Signs of the times were the opening of a New York club, 'The Sweet Chariot', dedicated exclusively to gospel music, and a *Melody Maker* article by Max Jones, entitled 'Gospel Truth or Pop Slop' (part of an immortal series that has included such gems as 'Skiffle or Piffle?', 'Folk or Fake?,' 'R & B Boom – Trend or Tripe?' and 'Blue Beat – new craze or old hokum?'). This was also the year when many people first became aware of Bob Dylan; and Peter, Paul and Mary informed the world that teenagers were sick of the pseudo and that they, Peter, Paul and Mary, sang 'folk songs of social significance'. But it was true that people wanted to hear something fresh – and freshness Dylan, The Beatles and Motown all had in abundance.

To say that Motown music was gospel-influenced is not to say anything very precise. For one thing gospel has always been influenced by the popular music of its day. While the blues can up to a point be regarded as a self-contained and self-subsistent form, in which traditions are passed on from one bluesman to another, it would be hopelessly misleading to discuss gospel music in glorious isolation. Then, styles of gospel singing are quite extraordinarily diverse, and only some of them are relevant to Motown. It is interesting, for example, to compare The Famous Ward Singers' version of *Who Shall Be Able To Stand* with The Sensational Nightingales' *God's World Will Never Pass Away*. The first performance is strongly reminiscent of swing styles, both in the accompaniment and in the singing. The soaring voice of the lead singer is backed by the chanted phrase 'great day' in a manner reminiscent of a swing riff. The lead singer carries the melody line and the role of the other members of the group is to echo and amplify. In The Sensational Nightingales' *God's World*, on the other hand, after an introduction which is highly secular in style, the backing group lays down a continuous chanting of the words 'never pass away' which builds up increasing tension and excitement and against which the lead singer shouts in a quasi-improvised fashion. The climax of the performance is reached when it is the *lead* who echoes the words of the accompaniment. Anyone who is familiar with the work of Levi Stubbs with The Four Tops, or of David Ruffin with The Temptations, will find The Famous Ward Singers foreign but feel at home with The Sensational Nightingales.

It is very important to recognise that the influence of gospel on black Americans is quite different from that of, say, Charlie Parker or John Coltrane on a European jazzman. The European listens self-consciously to and copies his model; the black musician, however, is exposed from his earliest childhood to the music of the church. He acquires a 'gospel sense' automatically, almost instinctively. Thus, once the taboos which confined gospel to its spiritual context were broken down, it was clearly only a matter of time before it percolated through popular music. It is meaningless then, in speaking of, say, the use of hand-clapping on a pop disc, to talk about 'pseudo gospel', since this is to invoke a purity that never existed, and to suggest that any kind of musical alteration or fusion is automatically false. If that were true, New Orleans jazz would have been the most debased form of music that had ever existed.

Motown music of 1963–4 was characterised by a gospel beat, in which the snare drum, prominently recorded, accented every beat and was reinforced by tambourines and hand-clapping. The result was a rhythm which, if potentially rigid, was nevertheless clear, rapid and danceable. However, its use at Motown had its own distinctive signature. The clarity and precision of the beat in gospel music is necessary if there is to be a firm foundation for the shifting vocal patterns. In much gospel music the vocal line tends to flow over the beat rather than remain strictly tied to it. But at Motown two main styles can be discerned. One, that of Martha and The Vandellas, is to come down heavily and emphatically on the beat in a way closer to rhythm-and-blues; the other, associated chiefly with Diana Ross, is to phrase more flexibly either against or over the beat in a manner which is superficially analogous to jazz singing. The traditional gospel flow can perhaps best be seen in the singing of Smokey Robinson with The Miracles, but his style is so personal and original that it cannot easily be categorised.

Another important element was the relationship between lead singer and backing group. Close-harmony vocal groups try to alter the texture of a consistently dense ensemble of voices. The Motown groups are quite different; their texture is much more open; the lead singer works against rather than with the group; there is a continual shifting between sections in which backing figures are sung behind the verse and ensemble passages in which the lead singer and group combine to sing the chorus. The Motown Spinners is a group that has attempted, not wholly unsuccessfully, to combine both styles; but their work does illustrate the difficulty of crossing over from one style to another. But the gospel style at Motown is infinitely more flexible. The reciprocity between lead singer and backing group makes it far easier to raise or lower the intensity of a performance. Gospel music is inherently dramatic, and in gospel performances extremely effective use is made of crescendo-diminuendo-crescendo-diminuendo patterns. In fact it was this more than anything else that made Ray Charles's performances of *A Fool For You* and *I Got A Woman* at Newport appear so striking.

The Spinners are Bobby Smith, Perris Jackson, Edgar Edwards, Henry Farnbrough and Billy Henderson. Their first hit was That's What Girls Are Made For *(Tri-Phi 1001) on a label owned by ex-Motown writer and producer Harvey Fugua.*

The significance of this in Top Thirty terms cannot be over-estimated. In the early '60s fans were beginning to forget the old division between ballads and beat numbers. Thus, in an article on Elvis in the *New Musical Express* (26 May 1960) Derek Johnson wrote:

Elvis is being shrewd in going along with the tide. For the demand for crude rock in large saturating doses no longer exists . . . Today the fans are more anxious to acknowledge the existence of melody; they like their basic rock in smaller doses and, generally speaking, would rather hear the beat dovetailed with a good tune.

The result was the ballad with a beat; but even this was a rather narrow formula. It was Motown group singing that pointed the way towards a record with a more complex structure, and songs like *The Tracks Of My Tears, Reflections* and *Yesterday's Dreams* fit into no pre-existing category.

To illustrate the scope of these changes let us take a disc from the Top Thirty of summer 1970, Ray Stevens's *Everything Is Beautiful*, which was extremely popular despite a melodic theme of quite extraordinary banality. After this theme has been sung by a children's choir, it is then taken up by the featured singer, whose voice is given a good deal of echo and is accompanied only by a light, rhythmic strumming. This rhythmic accompaniment is progressively magnified; the strumming becomes louder, and there are associated brass figures; piano and then organ amplify the texture and the brass is given more prominence; finally, half-way through the disc, singer and choir work in unison. Next, they sing antiphonally; the texture lightens as the singer is accompanied only by rhythm and piano; an organ swells the sound again, there is another crescendo, unison singing, a cry of 'one more time', etc. These constant variations in volume and texture keep the ear interested. The record appeals to listeners who probably do not much like most of what Motown puts out; and yet it relies on gospel devices which Motown and Ray Charles have popularised. For the hit record, like the advertising commercial, must make maximum use of its limited time, and, the more its contents are broken down and subdivided into identifiable segments, the more likely it will be that the record will achieve the greatest possible impact. Of course, records that repeat the same words over and over again can still make an impression through the sheer force of repetition, but commercially they are always more of a gamble.

At this point gospel simply becomes part of popular music in general, and it is not hard to understand the resentment which this facile acceptance arouses in devotees of the blues. Gospel appears as a kind of musical vodka, pure and clear, leaving no after-taste or hangover, blending with anything from country-and-western to pop, while the blues is a home-distilled sourmash whiskey, too potent, too idiosyncratic, too much an acquired taste for general consumption. Undoubtedly there does seem to be some kind of deep-seated taboo against the blues, whose concern is with failure, defeat and despair, whose anger and explicit eroticism are far removed from the euphoria and wish-fulfilment which Tin Pan

Alley has traditionally dispensed. Motown was able to circumvent this particular roadblock, but it has nevertheless brought a strength and directness to popular music that was hitherto lacking.

It is also characteristic of Motown music that it gives the chorus or refrain a more important position in the structure of a song. Rather than following a 32-bar pattern, repeated over and over with different words, the song is cleanly divided into separate sections of verse and chorus, each verse serving as a bridge between repetitions of the chorus. Such songs appear to move not in a straight line but in a circle. Usually they do not come to a definite conclusion but fade out over a chorus which is freer and more improvised than anything which has preceded it. The Miracles' *Shop Around* was the prototype of this song, and undoubtedly Smokey Robinson was the person responsible, either in his own right or as an influence on others working at the Hit Factory, for this new method of writing. To the casual listener these songs appear extremely simple, but when analysed they often prove surprisingly intricate. Jon Landau refers pejoratively to an a-a-a structure, but actually it is the conventional song which has this form; a song by The Miracles may well have the shape a-b-a-b-c-b. As I have already pointed out, it was rock 'n' roll that set in motion the shift from sheet music to disc.

Jamie was a hit in 1961. Later Holland joined his brother Brian and Lamont Dozier to form the renowned songwriting team.

Records from Freddie Gorman and Eddie Holland, both singers typical of Motown's adaptability.

But Smokey Robinson's songs seem to be the first that were specifically composed for the three-minute record. Sheet music is rather impersonal; anyone may play it, with virtually any combination of voices or instruments. Motown compositions, on the other hand, are designed for performance by a specific group, in a particular way, to achieve maximum impact on a three-minute side.

This is why it is necessary to talk about Motown *music* and not merely about a 'Motown sound'. From the beginning Motown established on Jobete an extensive repertoire of its own music. Berry Gordy, a songwriter himself, has always known the importance of good material. Also, Motown discs have been characterised by the deep involvement of their songwriter-producers – Smokey Robinson, Holland and Dozier, Norman Whitfield, Henry Cosby. The keynote has been adaptability. Eddie Holland and Barrett Strong are singers who have concentrated on songwriting, while songwriter Freddie Gorman has become a member of The Originals. This versatility – in the early days an economic policy – has meant that the best Motown discs reflect a concept of music as a whole, not merely one, like Spector's, of 'sound'.

In 1964–5 Motown was far ahead of the rest of the music business, and it has taken some sections of it a long while to catch up, especially in respect of the decentralisation, personal attention and continuity that Motown took for granted. The notion that making a record was simply slotting together tune, singer and arrangement in a one-shot operation was not easily discredited. In the mid-'60s Motown went from strength to strength, largely because of the work of Holland, Dozier and Holland with The Supremes and The Four

Tops. But their success was creating problems for the future. They were able to refine and consolidate the main elements of the Motown style into a consistent formula. They minimised the element of risk by their skill in fashioning variations on a theme, and they knew just what type of material was best for each group. With The Four Tops they helped to make some outstanding records, but with Diana Ross and The Supremes the limitations were more evident. It seemed that Diana Ross could make a hit of any song which alternated a jazzy, half-sung, half-spoken verse with a hammered-out refrain, but The Supremes' material began to lack variety. A typical reaction to later Motown (though not a Holland-Dozier-Holland production) was this *New Musical Express* review of The Temptations' *All I Need*:

I'm just a wee bit worried lest – with its sensational impact – the Motown sound might drive itself to saturation point. This one from The Temptations is absolutely typical of the Tamla output – exciting, dynamic, vibrant, irresistible. It flows along without pause, carried by its forceful toe-tapping beat. Features the inevitable solo vocal with chanting plus background dancing strings. Excellent of its kind and great for dancing. But The Temptations would do well in future to vary their style a bit...

In 1967 people were becoming more critical of Motown. For one thing, it had been in existence for some years; then, there was the Stax-Volt studio in Memphis. Motown's success had opened doors for black music in general. Atlantic, for instance, who had seen their hold on the R & B market weaken, and had suffered a body-blow in the early '60s when they lost two best-selling artists, Ray Charles and John Coltrane, to ABC-Paramount, were specially anxious to regain their success. They took over Stax-Volt and by 1966 were beginning to make an impression. One of the hits of that year was *Reach Out I'll Be There*; the other was Otis Redding's *Respect*.

The Memphis company was more closely in touch with mainstream R & B and in Otis Redding and Sam and Dave it had two outstanding acts. But Stax's major developments were in rhythm and arrangement. It is interesting, for example, to compare Sam and Dave's version of the Hayes-Porter song *You Don't Know Like I Know* with anything that Motown was doing in 1965. It is immediately evident that the Sam and Dave performance has a more relaxed and flexible beat and that there are more cross accents. Guitar, bass and drums are in rapport rather than rigid unison. While a Motown song sounded as though it were spinning endless

Otis Redding and (right) Sam and Dave.

circles, a Stax number thrust relentlessly forward with driving brass riffs, Otis Redding or Sam and Dave enthusiastically urging things on. Not that all the Stax records were better; but in the beginning they sounded fresher and less mechanical and, in a jazz sense, swung more.

Stax has undoubtedly left its mark, albeit indirectly, on Motown. The older company clearly decided not to compete but to carry on with its own music as best it could. Faced with the choice of going back into gospel, adopting Memphis-style soul, or directing its attention to a larger, non-rhythm-and-blues audience, it elected to play safe and widen its appeal. It could, in fact, have made no other choice. Gospel hand-clapping now seemed out of date, and the brass riffs on Motown's group records tended to make them sound too cluttered. So in 1967 The Four Tops were singing quasi-

ballads like *Yesterday's Dreams* and *I'm In A Different World*. But Detroit has also tried to give its records more rhythmic variety. Bongos and other exotic percussion effects have been used to provide rhythmic interest and contrasting textures. (Interestingly, this has also occurred in gospel songs, like The Famous Ward Singers' *Who Shall Be Able To Stand,* cited earlier.) Motown now has some excellent bass players, and on a disc like The Four Tops' *It's All In The Game* a clearly articulated bass line can be heard even on a portable radio or record player – which would have been unthinkable, despite multi-tracking, on sides of the 1963–4 period. There have been gains as well as losses in Motown's progress from then to now.

On the whole Motown has come through this period of adjustment remarkably well. The organisation is large and resourceful enough to ride through any changes of fashion in popular music, even though it is potentially more vulnerable than most. It is both

c

Stevie Wonder, born 13 May 1950, shown on one of his British tours.

less conservative – for it can attempt things that would have been musically or financially impossible in the early days – and more conservative, in that it has felt the need to consolidate the position of its own labels and artists, and now tends to respond to changes and innovations rather than initiate them. Motown has achieved a brand-name recognisability in popular music that is almost without parallel; but it is an open question whether it will continue to be identified with a particular kind of music, or, as seems more likely, will diversify and become just another record company, producing a widely varied output and hedging its losses.

As a company Motown has always been marked by a very strong orientation towards success. There is a reckless, almost quaint bravado, reminiscent of Gilded Age America, in the little house, heroically labelled 'Hitsville U.S.A.', where it all began. (Perhaps there will be a Hollywood movie one day.) Motown, as a small independent, had inevitably to project itself as successful in order to become established, and success is still the prominent feature of the Motown image. The *Blues & Soul* booklet *The Motown Story* uses the words 'success' and 'successful' at least thirty times. It is implicit, too, in the names of some of Motown's leading acts – The Supremes, The Four Tops, The Miracles, Stevie Wonder (born Stephen Judkins). At an early stage there was a policy of putting Motown acts into the fashionable night-clubs and cabaret restaurants. In an interview in the *Melody Maker* (19 September 1964) Mary Wilson was reported as saying:

We want to get into the night-club field and we know we're going to have to change our style a good bit to get there. We're working on that kind of singing now. We tried it out, our act that is, in a club in Bermuda last month.

I know there's a lot of work ahead of us but we really hope to play the Copa some day.

Not only did they do so – they have become the quintessence of what the Copa is all about. Today The Supremes, The Temptations, The Four Tops and Stevie Wonder have no difficulty in filling such engagements. It would be easy to criticise this policy from an ivory tower and, of course one cannot know how much stylistic modification has been necessary, but the fact remains that the leading Motown groups have achieved a durability and income that would almost certainly have been denied them otherwise; particularly since white youth, as in the days of High School music, prefers groups which reflect its own values and serve as its cultural representatives. The Motown acts have done vastly better than their predecessors; The Coasters, according to Phil Spector, never made more than $150 a week. Appearing like a ladder out of the restricted R & B market, Motown serves as a constant reminder that black artists can be successful. The expensive, glittering costumes worn by The Supremes, the colourful 'threads' of The Temptations, are visual proofs that the groups really have made it.

Nevertheless, there are risks in this policy. One, which has been averted perhaps because Motown is acutely conscious of it, is that in playing to relatively affluent and largely middle-aged white audiences the groups will lose touch with the teenagers and black Americans who buy the records. A more insidious threat is presented by the 'standards', the staple fare of night-clubs like the Copa. Motown groups can perform these numbers reasonably well without seriously compromising their style, but they sound far better doing their own numbers or others from the Motown repertoire. The songs of Gershwin, Rodgers and Hart or Irving Berlin obviously represent excellent music of an earlier style, but The Four Tops cannot get much out of them. Motown seems

The original Supremes, Florence Ballard, Mary Wilson and Diana Ross, and (right) Martha Reeves and The Vandellas.

strangely reluctant to acknowledge the strength of its own music and is notably deferential to the 'standards' of the past. The constellation of values is exemplified by the sleeve of 'The Supremes Sing Rodgers And Hart', where the various songtitles – *Thou Swell, My Funny Valentine, The Lady Is A Tramp* – are spelled out on illuminated neon signs. These songs are associated with a certain kind of glamour, with which The Supremes, in turn, must be identified. Similar thinking lies behind other Motown albums. The company still concentrates on singles, and most Motown collections consist chiefly of chart numbers or are of the 'Greatest Hits' type. Ideally, most of the songs on a new album would be new, specially written material, and occasionally they are, but more frequently the LPs are padded out with nondescript 'standards' and current hits like *Little Green Apples* – an example of 'creative' songwriting at its mushiest and most inane, which has regrettably been recorded by at least three Motown groups. But what is chiefly to be deplored is that these songs are on the whole so carelessly chosen, and so little is done with them. Through creative reinterpretation a number with no outstanding qualities can be utterly transformed and made to bear the individual stamp of the artist who sings it. Isaac Haye's version of the Bacharach–David number *I Just Don't Know What To Do With Myself* has this distinction, but Motown examples are all too rare, though Shorty Long's *Memories Are Made Of This* springs to mind. Motown is slowly sinking under the weight of the glittering dowry it has received, after persistent courtship, from

America's showbiz nobility; sooner or later the Hit Factory will have to recognise that these swing-era songs are more of a liability than an asset. They damage the integrity of Motown music and offer nothing in value in return. To this extent Motown is still the prisoner of its own self-image.

When Motown began, its attempts to reach white audiences – and so, indirectly, to break down barriers between black and white – put it in the mainstream of black American opinion, which, under the leadership of Martin Luther King, was still very much concerned with integration and racial harmony. Since then the idea of Black Power, however interpreted, and the new role of pop music as an outlet for white American dissent have made Motown and its tuxedo-clad artists seem both square and Uncle Tom. The most determined effort to combat this has been made by Norman Whitfield, working with The Temptations. The departure of David Ruffin from the group made it possible, and probably necessary, for them to change their image. Introducing an element of mystery, the album cover of 'Puzzle People' transformed the listener's potential uncertainty about the group into something positive. The group were taken out of their tuxedos and put into clothes which stressed their individuality and hinted at rebelliousness, unorthodoxy, the exotic. They were given songs which showed a greater concern with black identity, while their 'funkadelic' accompaniments aligned them, at least superficially, with innovatory tendencies in pop music. This new image, however, so dissimilar to the old, looks

Sleeves for albums by The Temptations: before and after.

somewhat synthetic, while the backings seem merely an exotic dressing – soul food with mango chutney.

At the moment, temporary successes at Motown have had the dubious effect of concealing fundamental problems. Originally its people were able to do what they did because of the rapport and understanding that were possible among a small number of vocal groups and composer/producers. Since then there have been too few new faces. Gladys Knight and The Pips and Edwin Starr were taken over from other companies (Starr was apparently the sole survivor of the Golden World label) and essentially Motown still relies on the same half-dozen or so acts which it had at the beginning. The Jackson Five have been the only real discovery in years, and it would be pleasant to think that Motown could also find acts that were over 13. Today the company is the successful tip of a very large iceberg of black music. In theory, in capitalist society,

38

Motown should be concerned only to return a profit to its stock-holders. In practice, as a major outlet, it owes it to the black com-munity, and perhaps also to itself if it is to continue to grow creatively, to develop and give exposure to more forms of black music. Today Motown seems behind the times in denying its artists more control over their careers. White rock is doubtless often posturing and pretentious, but its musicians are free to play almost anything they like – a freedom hardly shared by the Motown groups, who are brusquely marched up and down the Hit Parade-ground by sergeant-major-like composer/producers. And what was progressive five years ago now seems reactionary. Motown's obsession with the charts, and its emphasis on singles, has at least helped to keep the music direct, and discs like *Up The Ladder To The Roof* and *Signed, Sealed, Delivered* prove that Detroit has not lost its touch. Not, that is, with the charts – but what about the world outside the walls of the sound studio? Motown will have to open the doors if the promise of black music is finally to be fulfilled.

39

IT'S AN R'n'B INVASION

SUCCESS THRILLS

SUPREMES

Motown Record ... Seeks Distribution In Foreign Countries

THE MIRACLES will be ...

MOTOWN REVUE HERE NEXT YEAR

Tamla-Motown stars definite for February

STARS from America's fabulous Tamla-Motown Revue — including the biggest names in the R and B field—are definitely coming to Britain in February! Dick Katz of the Harold Davison Agency fixed the deal on his recent trip to the States and told DISC on Tuesday that the artists involved would probably be The Supremes, Martha and The Vandellas, Kim Weston and Earl Van Dyke, Marvin Gaye and The Miracles.

'Love' is Mr. Gordy's key to success

By MAUREEN CLEAVE

THE Beatles have done terrible things to the American record industry. Nobody knows what to record any longer.

The only company that knows what it is doing is a very small concern in Detroit called Tamla Motown.

Should they try to reproduce what is quaintly called the English Sound? Should they find a sound of their own? Should they resurrect Elvis Presley and Frank Sinatra for the teenagers?

CHARMING

With Tamla Motown you have Marvin Gaye, Stevie Wonder (Little Stevie Wonder), Martha and the Vandellas, the ... Temptations, the Marvellettes and (less abstract) the Con-tours.

Tamla Motown, with its associates, is said to be worth about nine million pounds. Last year it was the third most successful record com-pany in America; and one of the smallest.

It has taken Berry Gordy Junior, President of the Cor-poration, five years to build it up.

He is 34, a small, neat, well-dressed and completely charming person.

Many people stare at him, wondering how he does it. In their hundreds they come for auditions. They put their ears to the keyhole of his recording studios hoping to pick up a few tips. Mr. Gordy invites them in to listen, but they go away none the wiser.

Everybody who sings or works for Tamla Motown gets on with everybody else.

If the Miracles are through the studio while the Marvellettes are making a record, they help out with clapping. They all write songs for each other and they are mar-ried to each other. One ... a Marvellette, while one of the Marvellettes is married to a Contour.

Mr. Gordy is second young-est of a family of eight. Six of his brothers and sisters work in Tamla Motown. His sister, Mrs. Edwards, his other sister Loucey (married inci-dentally to Marvin Gaye) and Smokey Robinson (of the Miracles, who did so much for Mary Wells) are all Vice-Pres...

can go into any church choir and find talent, but not everywhere do you find hum-ility and a warm heart. That takes character."

Discipline is quite strict. Mrs. Edwards gives advice to the girls on how to dress and behave. "Mrs. Edwards is very particular about the way they look. She coaches them along and tells them how to conduct themselves. She is also concerned with their diet and their health on the road. She doesn't like them eating hot dogs instead of eating good." Edwards likes the fans ...

Hitsville, U.S.A. Helps Murray 'The K' Win New York's Second Battle of Rock

The stage was set in two different locations. Disc jockeys of station WMCA headlined their Paramount Theatre attrac-tion with "The Animals," while Murray "The K," WINS station chose Marvin Gaye to star in his Fox Thea-tre Revue in Brooklyn, across river.

This was the 1964 battle of New York "giants"—round New York ... Sid Bernstein, one of the promoters ... 'for the proceedings ... beat our pants off last East ... all by himself. Here we ...

'Baby Love' THE S...

AMERICA is back at the top. The Brit-ish beat stranglehold has been tem-porarily halted. The theory that ... achieve huge fame has ...

FIRST they hit num-... "Our Love Go?" ... beat that has ... Wilson ... British ...

Temptations bid for the top

RECORD ROUND-UP

SUPREMES make history

"THEY'RE number one!" I said. Apart from the crackle on the line, there was silence. Then a gasp. Then: "That's WONDERFUL! Just tremendous!" And in the Tamla-Motown offices, Mrs. Esther Edwards, vice-president of the company, shouted to the people nearest her: "They've made it! They've really made it!"

The Supremes, one of the label's hottest groups this week take over the No. 1 slot of the NME Chart ...

Page 10—MELODY MAKER, November 14, 1964.

MORE LANDINGS IN THE POP INVASION

Atlantic ... I'm told it makes pop h... both sides of the ... all-girl group has topped both charts ... Berry Gordy has probably break ... Britain to them when he comes ... Michigan ...

TOP U.S.

NME TOP THIRTY

Supremes o... ro-scherp...

...s you what to ...t R'n B stars

Kim Weston on Gerry too
KIM WESTON, accompanied by the Earl Van Dyke Quartet who were to have added to the Chuck Berry's ...

14 OKTOBER 1964
E TELEGRAAF

STORM IN

—dates anno...

AS America strengthene... British hit parade this w... announced for a three-wee... one of the most powerful U.S. pop p... Tamla-Motown recording stable. Beatles favourites Martha and the Vande... Gaye, and the Miracles are among artists se... plunge into Britain's top radio and TV shows in... few weeks.

...THAT GREAT... CALLED TAMLA-... MR. BERRY GORDY, JN... URAGED TO SCREAM AND YEL... OUR SENSES SHATTERE... TIME. THE REASON? A VISIT BY... VERY UN-BRITISH-LIKE WAY IN F... TAMLA-MOTOWN REVUE.

In February... The Supremes, M...

...'t rely... has a... t's like... y goes... brassy... works. "You... On Me"... audience... at you'd... hold o... will

WHAT THE PAPERS SAID

SUPREMES SUPREME!
Girls hit the top—and America scores again!

AMERICA is gaining impetus in the British hit parade. THE SUPREMES this week became the second U.S. act to top the chart in the last two years. They knocked Roy Orbison from the top spot with their second big hit, "Baby Love."

Orbison was first to smash the British beat stranglehold on the top spot. He did it with "It's Over" and followed up with "Oh Pretty Woman."

...the Supremes—Detroit's Diana Ross, ...ce Ballard—have se... be heavily-publicised

Tamla-Motown stable. It is the first number one hit from... company in Britain. The Supremes did it in four... entered at 31, while their first... "Where Did Our Love Go?" was ri... Then "Baby Love" wa... It was number th... The Supr... weeks...

The... original... Mr. Post... standard... Barrett St... recorder o... the origina... "a sou... has been around... instinctive is on me... one day be a... own right all... amla - Motown... ciety" in England... jodin, of 139... bexleyheath... dicts... an American,... B." the inst... beat are... their day... I am su... who have... appreciate... sound will... exactly wha... the Gordy st... On LP... SL... guy,... with

...que les aveugles cher... facultés musicales exce... doute parce qu'ils cherchent... compenser le manque d'ima... préhension sonore du monde... port un toucher aiguisé

labic names, if spoken suddenly... the response "hit records—top stars—big money." ...rds? You ought to have guessed it, for these names are ...g similar associations over here, but for all Record ...out-it" readers, they are: Tamla, Motown and Gordy. ...e field still further, try these names for... e Supremes, Martha and the Vandellas... g, the Contours, Eddie Holland. The... so on, almost ad infinitum. The... fact, the record companies which reco... d chartbusters.

...yr. is the name of the... He is president of... ...ation controlling the... and is proud to say... ...I started it... OUTLET... Berry started four... and since then 80 pe... releases have made t... charts. It was only... British outlet... Stateside label, si...

The Detroit sound forms a beach-head
BY BOB DAWBARN

BRITAIN exported the Liverpool sound to America—now America is sending us back the Detroit sound in the shape of Tamla Mo... own artists.

Martha and the Vandellas all from Detroit

NIGHT
2 4 OH, PRETTY WOMAN Roy Orbison (London)
8 5 HE'S IN TOWN Rockin' R...
3 LAST KISS

MARVIN GAYE

MIRACLES "extraordinaires" DISCO-REVUE

...istre pour la firme Tamla est absolument extraordinaire. Plusieurs ...et particulièrement « SHOPPING AROUND ». Bientôt va paraître ...prétation très appréciée aux soirées 100 % Rock du Golf Drouot ...les sont sans doute pour beaucoup dans la façon de jouer des...

Tamla-Motown star Marvin Gaye, aged 24, has not had a hit in Britain. ...the advent of the Detroit pop boom, his name has been en-...ly hurled about by singers and fans, and his recording are be-...e popular. Marvin was in Britain last week for TV and radio ...He took time off to review some of the latest pop singles Maker and proved an intelligent, analytical commentator.

W: "I'd Off With-... ca). I would ...top twenty ...not sure

Paul raves over Tamla-Motown stars

PAUL McCARTNEY produced a pack of cigarettes, offered around the group and ...ding up a lighter said: talking to him... It hit me on the head concert in Leeds last That's how excited the ...ence was getting! ...eccably dressed as usual. Paul came across to talk to me. ...him what he thought ...the Tamla-Motown groups ...which are going down great guns ...in this country at the moment ...to go down well here. ...They're all exciting entertainers ...those Supremes ...during their trip. ...The odd thing is thought that these ...coloured singers aren't really ...appreciated by the white people ...in the States—they come over to ...Britain and are knocked out by ...the reception they get. It seems ...only their own kind that ...

THEY'RE STILL THE TOPS!
Supremes supreme again —

Motown & the Critics

Motown discs have for a long time been the subject of criticism in the musical press and elsewhere, on several grounds; that they are too similar, that they are too commercial, that they are not genuine rhythm-and-blues. Probably some of this criticism is an indirect compliment, in so far as it suggests that people have high expectations of Motown and are disappointed if they are not fulfilled; but much of the rest is unfair and inaccurate, and some comments merely reflect a state of general confusion in pop music.

Before we can discuss popular music fruitfully, we must know exactly what we are talking about. Are we referring to a variety of forms of musical self-expression, from guitar-playing to choir practice? Do we mean music that has a broad popular appeal, rather than that which appeals only to a relatively restricted audience? A poll might well reveal that the majority of the British population would prefer Vera Lynn singing *There'll Be Bluebirds Over The White Cliffs Of Dover* to The Four Tops' *It's All In The Game*, let alone to the latest work of Frank Zappa. Beethoven would be more popular than certain progressive pop artists. So, in practice, when we talk about pop music we mean primarily a world which is defined by commercial criteria and dominated by the inscrutable charts – which possess the majestic power of making or breaking an artist. And we mean music that is bought and listened to by young people, who are, overwhelmingly, the members of society who spend money on records.

The paradox of pop music is that, although it thrives on the promotion of different types of music – folk, soul, hard rock – the role of the charts is to neutralise and cancel out any particular tendency. Every record is a one-shot operation. It goes up the charts, down again, and out. No matter how popular it is the odds are that just over three months later not many people will be buying it. If a disc is extremely successful it will probably, in the end, dig a grave for the kind of music it represents, by generating hybrids and imitations and by forcing its maker – the singer or group – to follow it with an identikit replica. On the whole the forms of popular music are remarkably stable and highly conservative – they persist not merely for years but for decades – yet the charts are notably volatile. How can this contradiction be explained?

In the first place, the very concept of 'pop music' is essentially false, since it postulates an homogeneous audience. The agreeable myth is disseminated that all records in the Top Thirty are enjoyed by all listeners, and naturally those that occupy a high position are enjoyed more than those lower down. Yet those who buy records by Shirley Bassey, Val Doonican or Ken Dodd will seldom be those who will buy one by Stevie Wonder or The Jackson Five. The charts, as tallies of records sold, embrace a number of divergent and, up to a point, distinct audiences, though to do well a disc must obviously appeal to as many of them as possible. Thus a Motown record which is just under or just in the Top Thirty is probably selling largely to Motown fans, and to reach the Top Ten it will have to sell outside this relatively loyal public. The assumption that everybody likes Top Thirty records more or less indiscriminately is necessary partly because disc jockeys do not wish to alienate sections of their audience and partly because it induces a spirit of commercial participation, in which people 'keep up with' the current hits by buying one or two best-selling discs – much as one might 'keep up with' the news – and thus symbolically 'vote' for an artist or group. The process is more or less self-regulating. Disc jockeys can seldom make hits; constant plugging may get them into the Top Thirty. But not much higher. But they can keep in touch with their audience and preserve their own popularity by playing records that are going up the charts; and the whole 'Will they or won't they reach the Top Three?' business stimulates interest and, ultimately, sales. To play a record that is going down the charts, however, is at best a sentimental luxury, at worst a criminal act which prevents the introduction of new stock and restricts turn-over. This is the tragedy of the DJ (at least, of the DJ who plays only singles): he is expected to have tastes in music, and ostensibly makes his living by expressing them, and yet, in the end, they are irrelevant. Consequently he has only two ways of talking about a disc. The first is to say 'This will be a hit'. This means one of three things: 'I like it', or 'In my considered professional opinion this record will sell', or 'I don't like it but won't admit it in case it is a massive success'. The second is to say 'nice record, nice voice, nice backing, nice production' – which is the nicest possible way of saying that he thinks it is an awful record, which will be a ghastly flop, but doesn't wish to offend the sensitive members of the music business. Either way, his own opinion can only be expressed through a kind of code. In this situation, of course, the record is simply a product, and the use of value-words has nothing to do with musical worth, however defined. A good record is one that sells.

All possibility of a critical perspective has now been abdicated. What alternatives are there? The principal approaches can be categorised as follows:

(a) ethnic, traditional;   (d) mass-cultural;
(b) sociological;   (e) pop Messianism;
(c) political;   (f) rock

– though these are not mutually exclusive.

The ethnic, or traditional, critical perspective is directly opposed to commercialism in all its forms; it stresses authenticity and tends to distrust innovation. Music is evaluated according to the degree to which traditional modes have been preserved. Thus the music of Big Bill Broonzy is more authentic than that of B. B. King, who differs as much from his predecessor as does Eric Clapton from B. B. King. The emphasis on folk music and tradition is valuable in so far as it insists that, in the blues for example, there is something of real value to be preserved; the problem is that in practice there is an inability to distinguish between constructive innovation or creative renewal within a tradition and blatant dilution or commercialisation. The distinction should not be hard to see, yet time and time again the former has been presented as the latter. Moreover, it is constantly in danger of collapsing into absurdity, because the attempt to erect absolute criteria does not take into account the enormous range and variety of popular music. In the words of H. L. Mencken, 'tragedy is a theory slain by a fact'. Today we have 'moldy fig' rhythm-and-blues purists, yet only twenty-five years ago rhythm-and-blues was itself dismissed as a crude commercialisation of the pure blues tradition. Motown is described as not being 'genuine' rhythm-and-blues, a judgement which reveals an ignorance of the place of Motown in black music as a whole, and postulates an ideal definition of rhythm-and-blues, even though the term can be useful only as an all-embracing description of black popular music.

In opposition to this ethnic standpoint (which has always been favoured more in Europe, where listeners are remote from the realities of American life), though sharing some of its assumptions, is the sociological approach of Charles Keil in his book *Urban Blues*. Keil rightly rejects the 'moldy fig' attitude to B. B. King, on the grounds that King's music commands a large following among black urban audiences and represents a response to new conditions.

He stresses the integrative role in the community of the bluesman as a kind of modern shaman. But his emphasis on the 'in-group solidarity' of the black masses leads him to be suspicious of Motown, and he criticises Leroi Jones for suggesting that young jazz musicians should be listening to The Supremes, The Four Tops, Marvin Gaye and Martha and The Vandellas. Keil's sociological concern with the blues as communicating 'the negro experience' to negroes (in other words, with the blues as a form of self-consciousness) makes the appeal of Motown to a white audience automatically suspect. According to Keil 'the Detroit sound is a soft-spoken, refined, polished soul music', and, turning a phrase of Leroi Jones's on its head, he writes: 'The Detroit sound is the one negro-produced style that comes closest to being "the music of another emerging middle class" and a culturally integrated American middle class at that, at least to the extent to which white teenagers are committed to it.'

Several points require comment here. Motown can easily be identified with the black bourgeoisie, since Motown is an extremely successful black business. But for his point to carry more than rhetorical weight Keil would have to show – as I strongly doubt whether he can – that the appeal of Motown within the black community is confined either to the middle-class or to those aspiring to join it. Moreover, even if he could do so, he would still not have produced an assessment of Motown *music*. A purely hypothetical verdict on the audience is transformed into a verdict on the music.

In any case Keil's sociological viewpoint is vulnerable to political criticism. Passing over the obvious bias that enables him to contemplate with equanimity B. B. King winning a substantial white audience, we can argue that the bluesman's integrative role in black society (as Keil sees it) is reactionary, inasmuch as he reconciles people to their existing situation, reinforces and articulates the known truths of their experience, but does not suggest that this experience can be altered or self-determined. While I like B. B. King, I would reject the view that all music must always be called upon to play a political role. I would suggest only that, when the black community has been warped and twisted by its efforts to survive within the larger white society, then something more must be at issue than the mere continuance of that community in its existing form.

A political approach to music can, of course, take another form, by criticising, as Adorno and Marcuse have done, the repressive apparatus of capitalist society. On this view, in its classic form, pop music merely represents the manipulation, both for financial gain and for the purpose of social control, of a passive, serialised,

Martha Reeves and The Vandellas were signed by Berry Gordy in 1960. There first record was I'll Have To Let Him Go *(Gordy 7011).*

alienated public. There can be no question that this approach has a great deal more relevance than one which regards pop music as an expression of pure, unfettered creativity, since it concentrates upon structures and determining forces. But there is a good deal of concealed élitism in such views. If only the masses were set free they would like Schönberg – as they should! Adorno's theory that all popular music and jazz must inevitably be the same was self-confirming, since he never wrote about it thoroughly enough to become conscious of any differences. Under the cloak of abstractions, helpless in the face of uncongenial and ungraspable realities, Marxism became transformed into a tragic pessimism.

Equally élitist in its assumptions is the attitude which I have described as 'pop Messianism'. Here the aim is to 'talk up' and dignify pop music, to secure its admission into the cultural pantheon. Its strategists play upon the fact that those who have cast themselves in the role of arbiters of culture feel vaguely guilty about their ignorance of pop music, which they recognise to be a sociological phenomenon of some importance. The threat to their guardianship is resolved, as always, by co-operation. Both groups are happy to talk about The Beatles and Schumann in the same breath. For the prophets of pop this is the dignity and acceptance of which they have dreamed. For the guardians of culture it means that the name of the game is still the same. Not one of their assumptions about what is valuable or significant in music need be seriously questioned; by glozening lore, analogous to the reinterpretation of the Old Testament, The Beatles are lifted out of their vulgar pop music surroundings and found to conform neatly with precedent. The Beatles are duly legitimised – but where does this leave the rest of popular music?

More fruitful than musical politics of this calibre is the attempt to talk in terms of 'rock' rather than 'pop'. In this way the heterogeneity of the charts and the matter of a record's success become irrelevant. Rock music can be shown to have a history, a continuity and even, up to a point, a unity. Furthermore, rock musicians can be talked about, very much as film directors are, as *auteurs*. One requires only the existence of a strong, consistent and highly individual body of work, which can be evaluated in its own terms.

On closer inspection, however, 'rock' turns out to be not so much a critical method as a woolly principle of an inward-looking white youth culture. The music must be felt to be significant, intrinsically different from 'bubblegum music'. In other words, the rock ethic is also élitist, and the role of the 'rock' concept is to place hard rock on a cultural plateau, thus automatically excluding comparisons with musical manifestations assigned to a lower level. Is The Creedence Clearwater Revival's version of *I Heard It On The*

Grapevine as good as Bobby Taylor's, let alone Marvin Gaye's? The question is irrelevant, because the Creedence version is not *only* a vocal, and runs for over eleven minutes. It is assumed, in fact, that Bobby Taylor's recording is to Creedence's as the crustacean is to the mammal. Anyway, Creedence exists in an entirely different cultural ambiance; it relates to its audience just as Bobby Taylor relates to his, and value judgements are expressions of partisanship, like the whirr of rattles at a football game. Reputations are created out of endless trade-paper gossip, and depend more upon the creation of an image, or of notoriety, than upon any musical achievement. This white sub-culture responds strongly to anything that reflects its own experiences and evokes a 'shock of recognition'; its limitation is that it does not respond at all to what lies outside it. Ever narrowing its focus, and yearning for cultural leadership, it strives to make the interest of its adopted 'superstars' into its own. One blank mirror confronts another. The rock ethic assumes that the music to which it is devoted is somehow free from the commercial pressures which operate elsewhere in popular music. 'Rock' lies within a magic circle drawn by an élite which knows, because it defines, what 'rock' really is. In practice this approach cannot become criticism, because it postulates and asserts but does not argue; because the idea of criticism undermines the freedom which permits everyone to believe what he wants to believe – a freedom which is at the heart of the rock ethic.

These views have something in common: they are all likely to have very little time for Motown's kind of music, either because it is too deeply involved in the commercialism of the Hit Parade or because it is insufficiently pretentious. They also share an extremely doctrinaire approach; whole areas of popular music are sweepingly dismissed as simply unworthy of attention. People's inability to make a value judgement about pop music that will stand up to a moment's consideration is matched only by their propensity to prejudge. On one side the inane DJ who pretends to like everything; on the other, a dogmatic critic who sees only what he wishes to see, unwilling to face the fact that there is no one-to-one relationship between commercialism and bad music. Good records may sell well or poorly: the critic's task is to say which they are without reference to the sales figures. Popular music needs catholic and informed discussion, based on listening without preconceptions, yet possessing a memory which recognises the dangers of disorientated eclecticism and bland trivialisation, and knows real innovation when it sees it. Pop music and pop criticism are horses running in blinkers. If they were removed Motown would be only one of the beneficiaries.

Come And Get These Memories

Martha Reeves & Smokey Robinson

After a time most records only sound older, tireder and very much flatter. That novelty intro now creaks like an old wooden door; the arrangement festoons singer and song like a gigantic cobweb, unable to conceal their fundamental tawdriness. Which is only to say that, in the perspective of time, even pop music acquires standards. In a context of imitation, duplication and endless retreading the truly original disc stands out with the purity of a Platonic idea. There is a tiny handful of records that not only do not date, but actually seem to get younger, exposing by their very freshness the stale unimaginativeness that has succeeded them. Among these are the early records of The Beatles, the classic sides of The Miracles and of Martha and The Vandellas, like *Come And Get These Memories, Dancing In The Street, Heat Wave, Shop Around, Way Over There, You Really Got A Hold On Me* and *Tracks Of My Tears.* Smokey Robinson and The Miracles, Martha Reeves and The Vandellas typify Motown in the age of innocence, and it is impossible to think of them without nostalgia. These groups created the identity of Motown music and despite the dictates of musical fashion they have remained true to it and to themselves. By comparison with some of Motown's acts their output has been relatively restricted – barely a third of what has been issued by The Supremes or The Temptations – while certain tracks of Martha and The Vandellas have cropped up on LP after LP, perhaps because it has been feared that people will not be interested in buying a record without a hit on it. But when judged by the acid test of the out-

Two hits from the early '6os.

standing single, which in the case of Motown is the only consideration that matters, both groups show up remarkably well.
They have been both the pioneers and the caretakers of Motown
music, paving the way for those who followed and setting standards
against which others could be judged.

It is fascinating to trace the emergence of a new music on their
early sides. They serve as a useful reminder that Motown did not
start as a vehicle of solid soul music and gradually degenerate into
commercialism. In fact the movement was the other way: they
began in the ambience of High School music and gradually dug
back into gospel and rhythm and blues. *Shop Around* sketches in
the figure of the dominating, possessive mother in a way that is
reminiscent of *Yakety Yak*, while *Mama Done Told Me* and *I Love
You Baby* are other numbers which find The Miracles in The
Coasters' country. In listening to Martha and The Vandellas, on
the other hand, one is struck by the group's ability to vary intonation and inflection. At times they sound unmistakably bluesy; on
other occasions, for example in *Can't Get Used To Losing You*, they
show themselves capable of reproducing perfectly the cute, coy, air-
conditioned style of white girl vocal groups. Similarly the importance of dance crazes is reflected in the curious contrast, in the output
of Smokey Robinson and The Miracles, between highly individual
songs that have become modern classics, like *You Really Got A
Hold On Me*, and discotheque numbers like *Come On Do The Jerk*;
between the complexity of *The Tracks Of My Tears* and the naïvety
of *That's What Love Is Made Of*. In the aftermath of Bob Dylan
such trivialities might seem contemptible, but it is as well to bear in
mind that a pop single is no more to be judged by its lyric than is an

50

opera by its libretto. Dylan may have dignified pop music, as Wagner dignified opera, but a great deal of excellent music has been written that makes no such pretentions. Criticism and discussion of popular culture invariably stumbles, by assuming either that popular art must be circumscribed by the social role which it performs or that it can be discussed without any reference to its specific context. At one extreme the Golden Bowl, at the other the Coca-cola bottle. Failing to examine the social co-ordinates of popular art is only an extension of the narrow aestheticism that sees the artist creating *ex nihilo*. Just as many black speakers have said that there is no 'negro problem', only a 'white problem', so, it could be argued, there is no popular culture problem, only an élite culture problem; the former is viewed through the distorting spectacles of the latter. Concern with the social morphology of art is regarded as tampering with the sacred mysteries; for to examine the conditions, whether permissive or repressive, under which art is created must ultimately be to question the bourgeois legend of the artist as conjuror or magician. By insisting on an artistic distinction between the sacred and the profane one does not preserve the integrity of art, one merely impoverishes critical discourse; for to speak of a 'good' discotheque record or a 'good' horror movie is to commit a solecism. The advantage of the term 'serious music', therefore, is that there is no obligation to show that serious music is good. Talking about Smokey Robinson threatens not Beethoven but Beethoven as a cultural totem; and if appreciating Beethoven means that profane music is to be drained of all value then the price is too high to pay. Criticism that is tied to a grazing post eventually ceases to be criticism at all. Why shouldn't we praise a record that is good for dancing not simply as good *dance* music but as good music? The recordings of Martha and The Vandellas are relevant here. It has become customary to speak slightingly of Motown's simple, danceable beat, as if the phrase defined its limitations. But if the beat is so simple, why is it that there are scarcely any records which even begin to approach the exuberant vitality and bounce of *Come And Get These Memories, That's When I Need You Most* and *Heat Wave*? Even Holland-Dozier-Holland, the original artists of mass-production, who composed these numbers and must therefore take a good deal of the credit, have not been able to repeat their achievements. But Western musical and cultural prejudices will not allow rhythm to be of anything more than secondary interest, subordinate to melody and harmony as the body is to the soul.

On the records of Martha and The Vandellas the contribution of The Vandellas is as important as that of Martha Reeves herself. The backing figures which they sing behind her provide the lift for her striding, loping style. The 'shoob doop be doops', 'uh-uhs' and

'ooh-ees' may be dismissed as childish gibberish, but they fulfil an essential rhythmic function. Unlike The Supremes, the group does not segregate verse and chorus; the lead voice is urged on by interjections that are rhythmic introjections, at once staccato and flowing, and the performance invariably builds to a climax as the vocal line is carried over a reiterated figure (*Heat Wave, Quicksand.*) It is interesting to compare these songs with a number like *Wild One*, which does not suit the trio because it is much more in the style of white girl groups, and in fact very plainly invokes the memory of The Crystals' *He's A Rebel*. On *Wild One* the chorus limply repeats the words with a delayed echo effect – 'what you wanna be', 'follow you,' 'security' – and the excitement created by shifting, incremental backing figures is wholly absent. But in *Heat Wave* two girls are able to create a blaring, biting accompaniment that has more power and precision than an entire orchestra. In *That's When I Need You Most* the title phrase is used as a sharply contoured riff, while in *Come And Get These Memories* The Vandellas sing the words 'since you got out of my life' with the surging flair of a Benny Carter-led sax section. The tonal spread of the ensembles, the tendency to slur a word across several notes, gives the group an attack that cannot be reproduced in mechanical unison singing.

On later records something of the original purity of this vocal style was lost. The use of heavy brass accompaniments, probably under the influence of Stax, in pieces like *Honey Chile* and *Without You* led to a kind of crude overstatement that was less interesting, and its temporary effectiveness was probably against the long-term interests of the group. On the LP 'Dancing In the Street' the re-recorded versions of some hits had a glossier, more brilliant sound, which was probably the reason for the deletion of the 'Greatest Hits' LP; but at least one performance, *A Love Like Yours (Don't Come Knocking Everyday)*, was a distinct disappointment. The original had found a relaxed and genuinely soulful groove which showed Martha Reeves' ability to invest a song with unmistakable blues feeling, but the second version sounded like a brash run-through of a number from the Motown songbook. In fact Martha and The Vandellas were one of the first groups to show that soul is a matter more of interpretation than of content. It was they who defined the Motown intersection between rhythm and blues, gospel and pop. But the charts have inhibited their capacity to develop, and only recently, in a number like *You're The Loser Now*

Martha and The Vandellas in 1970. Left to right: Sandra Tilley, Martha Reeves and Lois Reeves. Sandra Tilley came from The Velvelettes in 1969 to replace Rosalind Ashford, and Lois Reeves replaced Betty Kelley in 1968.

on the 'Sugar and Spice' LP, have they had a chance to show their capabilities.

It is difficult not to think of Smokey Robinson first and foremost as a composer, since, apart from the songs he has written for his own group, he has also been responsible for some of the most memorable numbers recorded by other Motown artists: *My Guy* (Mary Wells), *The Composer* (Diana Ross and The Supremes), *It's Growing* and *My Girl* (The Temptations), *Ain't That Peculiar* and *I'll Be Doggone* (Marvin Gaye). But if he had never written a bar he would still have become one of the most remarkable singers in popular music. His voice shows such fine control of vibrato, pitch and intonation, and such sensitivity to musical values, that one would be justified in saying that he used it like a musical instrument, were it not that no instrument could possibly imitate his expressiveness. His singing recognises no distinction between speech and song; it uncoils from a breathy, intimate whisper into a clear, bright, continuously intense verbal pressure. But perhaps most important of all is his sense of rhythm. He does not simply sing along with a beat behind him; he has a built-in sense of time which is really without parallel in popular music. One or two outstanding tenor players can pick up a saxophone and start swinging unaccompanied; one feels that Smokey Robinson could do just the same with his voice. This is what makes some of his dance records so delightful. The LP 'I Like It Like That', now regrettably deleted, is probably the best party or discotheque record ever made, and the beat in tracks such as *I Like It Like That* and the ridiculous *Groovy Thing* is infectious in the strongest sense of that maltreated word. While other singers land heavily on the beat, Smokey Robinson maintains a subtle, continuous contact with it – a kind of prehensile touching. He has shown that you do not have to shout and scream to be soulful, and that it takes more than muscle to swing.

Smokey Robinson and The Miracles have the ability to take any song and give it a tonal and harmonic colouring that is completely their own. Just as when Thelonius Monk plays *Sweet And Lovely* what comes out is all Monk, so when The Miracles sing *Hey Jude* they transform it into something that seems only distantly related to the original. But, of course, they are at their best singing Smokey Robinson's own compositions.

Robinson's songs are immediately identifiable by their unusual structure, their unexpected rhythmic emphases, their slowly moving, terraced chords, a fondness for the tonalities of G and D and their tortuous, suffocated melancholy. They focus almost obsessively on painful and contradictory feelings, on the discrepancy between dream and reality, between mask and face. Love is a 'guessing game' (*Doggone Right*). There is a need to turn dream into

Smokey Robinson and The Miracles: they recorded Tamla's first million-selling single, Shop Around *(Tamla 54034). Smokey Robinson's wife Claudette, originally a member of the group, left in 1965, but continued to sing on their records. Robinson is now vice-president of the Motown Record Corporation.*

You've Really Got A Hold On Me *(Tamla 54073). A Miracles'*
success in 1963.

reality (*Dreams, Dreams*) or to recognise an illusion for what it is
(*The Love I Saw In You Was Just A Mirage*), to come to terms with
the paradox that 'each hurt makes my love stronger than before'
(*Ain't That Peculiar*). The victim is placed in an intolerable position
of dependence (*You Neglect Me*), while in *The Tracks Of My Tears*

56

and *The Tears Of A Clown* the conflict between keeping face and inner feelings of despair becomes unbearable. *The Love I Saw In You Was Just A Mirage* and *The Tracks Of My Tears* create, by repetition, a hypnotic trance out of which the singer seems incapable of breaking.

The latter song is their masterpiece. It is composed of at least four musical elements; the gay, humming theme with which it opens is associated with the singer's self-confident public role, while the plangent refrain is linked with the painful feelings of his real self. The verse expresses, almost from the outside, the tension created by this discrepancy. The song moves towards a climactic recognition of failure – 'Outside I'm masquerading/Inside my hope is fading' and the pattern of stresses becomes more and more emphatic. The confessional character of the song is gradually intensified until it swells into an overwhelming incantation of masochistic self-humiliation – 'Baby, baby baby, take a good look at my face . . . Look a little bit closer now'. This is not simply a song but a powerful emotional statement.

The songs of Smokey Robinson are unusual in their integrity and their truth to experience. By comparison the work of, say, Irving Berlin, despite its distinctive musical thumbprint, is vapid and generalised; it has no conception of this kind of impersonal authenticity. With a touch of hyperbole Smokey Robinson could be described as the Petrarch of modern popular music, because he has taught artists, from Dylan to The Beatles, the relevance of the advice 'Look in your heart and write'. He, more than anyone, has made it possible for us to think of the popular song as a kind of poetry.

The Miracles as they were from 1955 to 1965, before Claudette Robinson left the group. The other members are Pete Moore, Bobby Rogers and Ronnie White.

The Supremes & The Temptations

Motown, like Chairman Mao Tse Tung, is wedded to a philosophy of 'going on two legs'; the principle is to keep one foot in the world of rhythm and blues and the other in the wider (or narrower) world of pop music. More out than in are The Temptations and The Supremes. The Miracles and Martha and The Vandellas have never strayed very far from the gospel-tinged music of early Motown; Stevie Wonder and The Four Tops, despite their broad appeal, seem never to forget that their roots are in rhythm and blues; but The Temptations and The Supremes appear to have no special allegiance. They can turn their hands to anything and everything, and in speaking of them 'versatility' can be taken as implying either criticism or praise. Points of contact between the two groups are numerous. Both are celebrated for their (literally) glittering night club appearances. In both, the identity of each member of the group is, and must be, subordinated to a carefully cultivated public image. Both groups have had to face the problem of adjusting to the loss of a key lead singer (David Ruffin, Diana Ross) and have managed, in different ways, to overcome it. The original association between The Temptations and The Supremes – some of the founder members knew each other well in High School in Detroit, when they were going under the names of The Primes and The Primettes–has been renewed in recent years by joint appearances and through record albums which they have made together. In the darkest hours of show business, when a chasm was yawning between the well-groomed celebrities of yesterday and the jean-clad idols of today and tomorrow, it was they who stepped in to fill the glamour gap and rework the fraying fabric of the American dream. High up in the Big Top they danced across a silken tight-rope that transcended all contradictions. The Temptations sang a song called *Slave* and appeared at the Copacabana in the outfits of

Mississippi river-boat gamblers. Diana Ross and The Supremes sang *Big Spender* and spoke of Martin Luther King. Alluding to the Motown slogan, 'the Voice of Young America', Chester Higgins wrote of The Temptations: 'They are, indeed, the voice of youth, and more. They appeal to mature audiences as well'. Reaching white as well as black, old as well as young, they appeared to fulfil a more than musical function; in the anxious and guilty America of the '60s the integrative role of these sequined shamans seems worthy of anthropological analysis. Not for nothing did Diana Ross, at the end of the decade, proclaim the dawning of the age of Aquarius – harmony and understanding, sympathy and trust abounding – and thereby appear to offer a resolution of America's problems that was both musical and magical.

The Temptations led by David Ruffin and The Temptations led by Dennis Edwards sound so utterly different that it seems logical to discuss them as if they were separate groups. This distinction is

reinforced by the fact that the original Temptations came into prominence through songs which were written for them by Smokey Robinson, who also served as their producer, while virtually all of the material for the group as it is currently constituted has been written by Norman Whitfield and Barrett Strong. Later discs by The Temptations have their merits, but one does not have to be a partisan of David Ruffin to feel that the classic sides recorded by this group are concentrated in the early years. The real gems are all Smokey Robinson compositions – *The Way You Do The Things You Do, My Girl, It's Growing.*

The style of the original Temptations was extremely romantic. Their songs were always tender, warm and affectionate; even those which dealt with the end of an affair expressed wistfulness and longing rather than anger or resentment. When they made *You Really Got A Hold On Me* they sang it well in their own way, but the astringency of the opening words, 'I don't like you, but I love you', went for nothing. A characteristic Temptations performance featured a steady, rocking tempo, a slowly building melodic line, and an intensity created gradually through rhythmic chanting, humming, crooning and shrill cries of 'Girl, girl, girl'. The Temptations were distinctive because they were not simply a lead voice with backing group but a constantly shifting formation of five matched yet individual voices, which served as a frame for the

The Temptations as they were from 1964 to 1968. Left to right: Otis Williams, David Ruffin (lead vocal), Eddie Kendricks, Melvin Franklin and Paul Williams.

unique rapport between the plaintive high tenor of Eddie Kendricks and the commanding vocal presence of David Ruffin, who could modulate at will from an ingratiating softness to a throaty, passionate shouting. Amid a host of carbon-copy Otis Reddings, David Ruffin is a singer whose outstanding ability has received all too little recognition. His experience in gospel groups such as The Dixie Nightingales and The Soulsters has enabled him to bring an unusual earnestness to the singing of secular love lyrics. In fact he can be compared only with Ray Charles in his ability to take the most threadbare ballad and turn it into a dramatic and completely convincing emotional statement. If ever The Temptations teetered on the brink of sentimentality, they were saved from it only by Ruffin's rasping, carefully articulated and deeply-soulful delivery.

Smokey Robinson too had an important hand in The Temptations' achievement. His compositions for the group are perfectly adapted to their style – though perhaps it could as well be said that he helped to create it. Many popular songs seem to do little more than mechanically assemble words and notes, but his are always personal and capable of creating a precise mood. A Holland-Dozier-Holland number is likely to impress the listener with the skill with which it has been put together, but songs like *My Girl* and *It's Growing* are all of a piece and cannot be broken down into their constituent parts. Their simplicity and directness are truly song-like. They employ only a very small number of chords, but acquire a cumulative, hypnotic power by the repetition of those chords and by their association with specific words. A Smokey Robinson song is always incremental; in *It's Growing*, for example, the simile 'like a snowball rolling down the side of a snow-covered hill' fits exactly. Again it is the chorus which plays the dominant role. The verse of this song, with its repeated comparisons, resembles that of a standard, but in a standard there would simply be other comparisons and that would be that. In *It's Growing*, however, the singing of the chorus takes up very nearly twice as much time as the verse, and the repetition of the phrase 'It's growing' in the verse, which is sung (unaccompanied) by David Ruffin, is only a prelude to the surging ensemble work of the chorus, where the continual reiteration of the word 'grows' over a clashing accompaniment powerfully embodies the meaning of the song. The relationship established between words, music and performance is so intimate, so subtle, that the majority of popular songs seem by comparison one-dimensional. *The Way You Do The Things You Do, My Girl* and *It's Growing* are imbued with such freshness, sincerity and glowing vitality by The Temptations that one feels inclined to wonder why there are so few genuine love songs, why the only available modes seem to be adolescent yearning or maudlin self-pity. It is only in black music

David Ruffin, from Meridian, Miss., recorded for Chess and Anna before joining The Temptations as lead singer in place of Eldridge Bryant. He left The Temptations in July 1968 and became a popular solo attraction.

that love is treated without falsity or self-consciousness.

At least, in some black music; subsequent Temptations' hits like the Whitfield–Strong–Penzabene compositions (*I Wish It Would Rain* and *I Could Never Love Another (After Loving You)*) are

SOUL
America's Most Soulful Newspaper

Volume 3, Number 17   December 2, 1968

Motown Wants David Ruffin Back
Company Busy At Work To End All Differences

DETROIT—Word from this city is that David Ruffin and Motown Records are about to patch up their stormy romance and remarry.

Ruffin, who is suing Motown for keeping him in peonage, is reported by sources close to the ex-Temptation to be one verge of dropping his litigation.

Motown Records, who received an injunction against the singer which prevents him from recording for any other company, is rumored to be on the brink of cancelling a suit against C. B. Atkins and Joe Glaser (Associated Booking Corporation) which claims that the two men induced Ruffin to leave the Detroit label.

If he and Motown get it together, David will remain a solo singer for the company. In the meantime, he's been gigging around the country, including a three day engagement at New York's Apollo, with a group billed as David Ruffin And The Fellas.

Motown has Ruffin under contract until 1972 as a solo artist.

... DAVID RUFFIN ON HIS WAY HOME
deep down inside does a voice ask "Where am I going, and what will I find?"

Tammi Terrell Alive, But Can She Return?

She's okay.

Tammi Terrell, l o n g rumored dead or dying, is planning to go back to performing as soon as her doctor gives the word — and she hopes to get it on Nov. 26 and be back into full swing shortly after Christmas.

In a long distance telephone interview from her home in Philadelphia, Tammi said "I'm feeling fine. I've been staying home and recuperating."

In June, she recorded the album "You're All I Need" with Marvin Gaye in Detroit, working 12 and 18 hours a day. Then she flew to the Bahamas for a vacation before returning to her parents home in Pennsylvania.

Tammi underwent exploratory examination some time ago for a brain tumor following a collapse on stage while p e r f o r m i n g with Marvin. She's been suffering from headaches and dizziness for many months.

Her doctor ordered her on a limited work schedule. Mostly, Tammi said, it's a matter of when she's tired, she rests. Otherwise she works.

During her recuperation, she picked up some hobbies. "I learned to knit in the hospital," she said, laughing. "I feel like a grandma." And she's been cooking and eating soul food. "Am I on a diet! I went down to 93 pounds in the hospital and now I weigh 125," Tammi added.

Her hair, shorn off for surgery, is "almost a natural now," she said. "For awhile there, my father said I looked just like him. Tammi Brenner!"

The one thing that's pulled her through her t r o u b l e s, Tammi added, is an overwhelming desire to get back to work. At first depressed at missing shows just when she and Marvin, as a team, became popular, she's gotten over it now and is spending her time either staying at home or going to parties.

Has Tammi learned anything from her blues? "I've got a lot more faith — in God," she said quietly.

... TAMMI TERRELL
taking 'time out to knit

Feliciano Releases Single of 'Star-Spangled-Banner'

LOS ANGELES, Calif. — When Jose. Feliciano sang our national anthem at the World Series recently some people protested, saying his "soul rendition" was in poor taste. But the folks who turned out at a recent Humphrey rally here gave him a standing ovation.

Feliciano had been asked by Humphrey, personally, to appear and sing The Star-Spangled Banner.

RCA Victor has since released a single of the controversial Feliciano's controversial arrangement thus adding more fuel to the fire.

In recent years this song has been the center of musical attention. First Robert Goulet forgot the words, Andy Williams sought to have it replaced by "America The Beautiful," then Aretha did it at the Democratic Convention in Chicago and the band was always two bars ahead of her. So far it has survived, but since Jose had done it, the only way he could, he later explained, one wonders, what next?

By the way, what do you do when you are driving along or walking down the street and you hear "Oh say can you see . . . yeah, yeah."

Troubled times for Ruffin and Tammi Terrell.

typecast lachrymose ballads, urgently in need of David Ruffin's talent for resuscitation. Pop-formula thinking is always impoverishing; it flattens a group into an unobtrusive noise that will blend happily with the flowing string figures. The use of recorded seagulls in *I Wish It Would Rain* ushered in an era of gimmickry: wah-wah guitars, chinoiserie and crashing gongs, and sound effects like the crying child of *Run Away Child, Running Wild,* the

Dennis Edwards (far right) replaced David Ruffin as lead singer with The Temptations in 1968. Previously one of The Contours, he heralded the new 'psychedelic' approach.

birdsong in *It's Summer,* the train in *Friendship Train* and the creaking door of the *Psychedelic Shack.*

With the departure of David Ruffin, The Temptations embarked on a quest for identity which has still not ended. The inclusion of Dennis Edwards precipitated changes more extensive than may have originally been contemplated. His gospel credentials were just as impressive as those of David Ruffin, but his natural tendency to sing against the rest of the group virtually eliminated its characteristic shading. At the same time, he tended to phrase heavily on the beat like a blues shouter. It is noteworthy that he has been at his best in bluesy numbers of the sort that also suit Gladys Knight – *I Heard It Through The Grapevine, That's The Way Love Is* and *Cloud Nine*. *Cloud Nine* suggested the possibility of a new and more insistent style for the group, in which Eddie Kendricks and Dennis Edwards would offset rather than complement each other. On the whole the 'Cloud Nine' album was not unpromising, and *Run Away Child, Running Wild* was an attempt – albeit not a particularly successful one – to go beyond the three-minute limit, in a manner that recalled Nina Simone's *Sinnerman*. But the 'Puzzle People' LP, sometimes cited as a meritorious instance of progressive soul, was a disastrous slide into Mickey Mouse music. The group's style was reduced to banal exchanges between tenor, baritone and bass, with mechanical unison singing and a beat so leaden that one could scarcely recognise the artists responsible for the exuberant swing of *The Way You Do The Things You Do*. Superficially progressive, under the influence of Sly and the Family Stone, the group actually retrogressed.

In *Psychedelic Shack* The Temptations finally caught up with Flower Power. From Norman Whitfield and Barrett Strong came 'message' lyrics of such crushing obviousness that it would be a compliment to describe them as the musical equivalent of a *Time* magazine think-piece. Pseudo-revolt concealed a fundamental complacency – war was bad because it had caused unrest within the younger generation! Damage was being done to the ideal of the docile, well-behaved teenager! Then, in *Hum Along And Dance*, Dennis Edwards' fierce cry 'there ain't no words to this song – people' reduced soul to pure expressiveness, devoid of meaning, devoid of soul. Such, for The Temptations, was the consequence of their determined attempt to keep in touch with the tastes of a predominantly white audience.

Similar forces have worked upon Diana Ross and the Supremes, though they were, from the very beginning, the most obviously commercial of the Motown groups, and their commercial potential was clearly recognised and exploited. The paradox of The Supremes is that while, in some senses, they are the least *typical* of Motown groups, they are at the same time the most *representative*. It is The Supremes of whom people tend to think when they hear Motown mentioned, and it is The Supremes whom even relatively well-informed critics usually have in mind when they are making their glib generalisations about Motown. Diana Ross, in particular, has a central role in the Motown image, reflected iconographically in *The Motown Story*, where she appears in a colour photograph on the

back cover, and then again on the front in large scale, rising out of the other groups like Aphrodite from the sea. Perhaps one might also see in this a symbolic transcending of the world of rhythm and blues.

The Supremes are probably the hardest Motown group to write fairly about, because it is difficult to know what criteria can reasonably be invoked. Yet this elusiveness makes their case all the more interesting; for they reveal most clearly how Motown's gospel-influenced music became refined into a chart-bound formula. The relationship between lead singer and group was gradually attenuated. Interplay within the group was transformed into a style in which the backing voices were used almost exclusively for reinforcement. Repetition had become the essence of the popular song – repetition of the disc itself through airplays, and repetition within the disc of a particular refrain. Diana Ross, in fact, established herself as the leading exponent of the recording-studio singing of the '60s. Her hard, bright tone and the penetrating high notes of The Supremes could almost have been designed for the transistor. The group was always disciplined, controlled and professional, able to achieve a perfect take in the shortest possible time. Diana Ross was able to thread her way dexterously through a complex and over-loaded arrangement, to deal effortlessly with changes in tempo, to shift accents, to mount waves of sound like a surf-board rider. It was impossible not to admire her tremendous verve and agility. But listening to her was rather like being subjected to the sharpness of a tattooist's needle; undoubtedly the effect would not wear off, but whether it was artistic was another matter.

Diana Ross's singing could be criticised as lacking in feeling and inner conviction, but in a way this would be irrelevant. Artistry can express itself in formal ways and her approach to a song was, like Sarah Vaughan's, almost exclusively technical – to show what she could do with it rather than to convey an emotion. If her singing was antiseptic and lacking in colour it was at least free from the false romanticism of much Top Thirty material. It is interesting, for example, to compare her version, with The Supremes, of *Put Yourself In My Place* with the original hit version by The Elgins, particularly since Saundra Edwards of The Elgins has a rather similar voice. The Elgins make the song into a resigned and sentimental ballad. It is taken at quite a fast tempo, but Diana Ross's instinct is always to push a number along and she sings it even faster.

Diana Ross, born 26 March 1944, sang with The Supremes from 1960 until January 1970. Her second solo record, Ain't No Mountain High Enough *(Motown 1169), topped the U.S. charts.*

The words *Put Yourself In My Place* are thrown down almost as a challenge and the lyric is given a strong, and very characteristic, flavour of sexual resentment. One of the paradoxes of Diana Ross's career, in fact, is that she made her name singing about being broken-hearted, betrayed and abandoned, yet this material now only undermines attempts to present her to white, middle-aged, night-club audiences as the successor to Eartha Kitt. It has always been a rewarding feature of her work that she sings about love in ways other than those conventionally ascribed to girl singers, thus challenging (despite occasional coy mannerisms) those outmoded and degrading feminine stereotypes.

The songs which Holland, Dozier and Holland have written for The Supremes provide the clearest illustration of Motown's assembly-line methods. These writers have never been able to resist having two bites at the cherry. If a song proves to be successful they invariably follow it with one on similar lines. They ruthlessly cannibalise old songs for spare parts; verbal phrases, thematic ideas, musical figures, accompaniments, even saxophone solos are shuffled together and reworked from disc to disc; every song is a collage. And the new combination usually works. The disc is sufficiently similar to its predecessor to satisfy the conservative instincts of the record-buyer, and sufficiently different to assuage his desire for novelty. Again, the forces at work are the usual commercial ones; the company must maintain a distinctive identity and yet, at the same time, continue to originate new products. In a pop music context this conflict continually verges on crisis for each artist is presented to the public with a unique identity, which must nevertheless be subject to yearly model changes. No wonder the music papers find so much to talk about even when they say so little!

In The Supremes' output there are four key songs: *Where Did Our Love Go?, You Can't Hurry Love, You Keep Me Hangin' On* and *Reflections. Where Did Our Love Go?* must be regarded as one of the classic records of the Motown take-off period. As The Primettes the group had shown themselves capable, in a number like *Pretty Baby*, of singing in a hard-driving manner reminiscent of Martha and The Vandellas, but to *Where Did Our Love Go?* they brought an attractive airy lightness. Diana Ross floated her singing of the lyric above the pounding beat and it was her phrasing that made the record swing. When she sings the words 'You came into my heart', the musicians, who have played a rather wooden introduction, begin to get into a groove. For all its ostensibly sad theme the song is quite surprisingly gay. The situation is aesthetically distanced and transcended through the dispassionate simplicity of the performance. *You Keep Me Hangin' On*, however, strives for a catharsis of a quite different kind, and is altogether more convincing

The Supremes in Britain, 1965: Florence Ballard, Mary Wilson and Diana Ross.

as an emotional statement, for the insistence that is so characteristic of The Supremes has here a genuine purpose – to exorcise the feeling of pain. The song describes the experience of being rejected in love. There is a kind of fatalism in the repetition of the title words and the jangling that accompanies them. The theme is that of a struggle to break out of a vicious circle, which can be achieved only by expressing, and therefore admitting, latent hostility. In the triumphant jeering of 'Get out – get out – get out of my life' the spell is finally broken.

The other two songs which I have singled out, *You Can't Hurry Love* and *Reflections*, depict an oscillation between contrasting moods. *You Can't Hurry Love* centres on the classic Freudian conflict of the pleasure principle and the reality principle; between the need for love and the need to accept the wisdom of Momma's good advice. The tension created by Diana Ross's urgent singing of the verse is continually alleviated by the altered tempo and the lilting rhythm of the chorus – 'You can't hurry love/You'll just have to wait'. This refrain serves almost as a motto theme, constantly returning and overwhelming a strong resistance to it. On the words 'I keep on waiting' it is heard as a kind of melodic warning in

Florence Ballard left in 1967 to record for ABC-Paramount, but without success. Right: The Supremes in 1970, Cindy Birdsong, Mary Wilson, Jean Terrell.

the accompaniment, and the song ends with the lesson learned and accepted as a truth of experience. *Reflections* is reminiscent of *You Keep Me Hangin' On* but the experience described is more complex. The use of electronic sounds is no gimmick but conveys aurally the importance of memory and the transitoriness of experience; the

sounds stand for the passing reflections, which in turn are images of the past. The song alternates between moody, introspective reverie, recalling happy memories of the past, and anger, upon realising that this fixation on the past is the reason why 'my world has turned to dust'. But the song remains obstinately retrospective. The conflict cannot be resolved.

By the late '60s Diana Ross had come to assume a dominant role within The Supremes, and it might have been expected that her departure to go solo would be as disastrous for the group as the loss of David Ruffin had been for The Temptations. The arrival of Jean Terrell, however, revitalised The Supremes and made *Up The Ladder To The Roof* their most electrifying disc in years. Superb mastering made the record positively explode against the limits of

The Supremes. Left: Cindy Birdsong, Diana Ross and Mary Wilson; right: Cindy Birdsong, Jean Terrell and Mary Wilson.

its dynamic range. Now the group had more bite in the ensembles, a surging power and directness that had been missing for far too long. The Supremes were back on the right track. Mary Wilson, interviewed in *Disc* (18 July 1970), said:

Basically we're still The Supremes as they always were. Some people expected drastic changes but really we've just gone back to the early Supremes sound. We're going to be more Rhythm and Blues and pop, not as sophisticated as the former Supremes were. We won't be trying to get into the night-club circuit.

The wheel had come full circle.

The Four Tops
The Same Old Song

In popular music most groups and singers fall into one of two categories. The minority remains faithful to its own kind of music, regardless of short-term popularity; the majority dissipates what little integrity or identity it has in a desperate chase to keep up with the latest trend. But there are a few talents which are virtually indestructible, which have such a clearly defined musical character that they can make compromises and concessions that would be ruinous to others and emerge virtually unscathed. To this select group belong The Four Tops. Broadway may not be their milieu, but they can go there and come back and remain just what they were before. They may not sound as good in *By The Time I Get To Phoenix* as they do in the songs written for them by Holland, Dozier and Holland, but the result is nevertheless very acceptable. For The Four Tops versatility does not mean doing different things in different ways, but doing everything in their own way.

The Four Tops are unclassifiable. They are equally at home in pop music and in rhythm-and-blues. They have shown that it is possible for Motown to aim at the Top Thirty or Fifty and produce music that is good by any standard. In the past, R & B records which reached the national charts in Britain and the United States tended to be those with some kind of novelty appeal, but in their pioneering work with Holland, Dozier and Holland The Four Tops have finally broken down the barrier between R & B and pop music – one would like to think for ever. The Four Tops themselves strongly resist any attempt to categorise their music. The *New Musical Express* (27 May 1967) reported Levi Stubbs as follows:

But he gets very angry at people who label the Four Tops as 'Tamla-style' or as 'a soul group'.

'We're not any one thing' he told me seriously. 'Over the years we've been lucky in being able to appeal to many various tastes in music and this is still our policy.

'I don't see why we can't make good commercial records and still have quality. We like to think we have something to offer everybody.'

Fifteen years ago The Four Tops were known as the Four Aims. They recorded for Singular, Columbia and Riverside before joining Motown.

A reasonable enough proposition. But the insistence of purists that an R & B record is an R & B record leads ultimately to the assumption that only white music can be universally popular – despite convincing evidence, in the '60s, of the reverse. Groups like Smokey Robinson and The Miracles, Martha and The Vandellas and The Four Tops have enjoyed great popularity without making serious compromises.

The Four Tops, like The Miracles, have been an extremely stable group; there have been no changes in personnel since they formed in 1954, and the group still consists of Levi Stubbs Jnr, Abdul Fakir, Renaldo Benson and Lawrence Payton. They resemble The Miracles also in their naturalness and lack of affectation; they do not rely on an artificially created image. Although theirs is not the most famous of Motown's stage acts, it is one of the best, and on the right occasion they are capable of communicating very strongly with an audience. Reporting their 1967 British tour Alan Smith wrote in the *New Musical Express*:

They were hardly half-way through their second number *Baby, I Need Your Loving* before thousands of us present were on our feet, joining in with all the fervour of a Saturday night at a Harlem Salvation Army meeting.

The Four Tops generate a strong sense of swing. On their early records there was a wonderful spontaneity and rhythmic flow, even though they were one of the last Motown groups to abandon rock 'n' roll-style backings; in later performances, with the Motown tambourine beat, the freedom and rapport created within the group ruled out any possibility of rigidity. Everything, however, depends on the contribution of the lead singer, Levi Stubbs. His singing rivets the attention by its magnificent sense of drama and by a power, not merely forceful, which, avoiding any suggestion of strain, verges on a kind of grandeur. He is not merely a shouter; his voice has a burnished, trombone-like sonority and his wide-spanning solo lines demand great confidence, imagination and musical intelligence. Although, in many Holland-Dozier-Holland numbers, the main lines of the interpretation are dictated by the character of the composition, it is nevertheless true that without The Four Tops the conception could never have been fully realised. Brian Holland was wholly justified in saying:

I don't think we'd have done so well without some great artists to perform our songs.

The Tops, for instance, are vocally brilliant. In fact vocal-wise they are my personal choice because I've got such a great admiration for their entire style and delivery.

(*New Musical Express*, 18 November 1967)

The Four Tops' records with Holland, Dozier and Holland combined the beat and soulfulness of R & B at its best with the attention to detail that was characteristic of the new pop music.

Since it was Holland, Dozier and Holland who demonstrated the

ARE SITTING AND WAITING

Left: Brian Holland; right: Lamont Dozier, who recorded under the name of Lamont Anthony on the Motown-distributed Melody label before becoming part of the songwriting team in the '60s.

possibility of pouring out an endless stream of assembly-line hits, they must be regarded as one of the most significant portents in popular music of the '60s. Brian Holland was reported as saying 'Songwriting's a job of work . . .We come in; we sit down; and we concentrate'; words which seemed to banish for ever the Hollywood myth of the impoverished, shirt-sleeved, sweat-stained songwriter, who, in the early hours of the morning, feverishly casts an empty whisky bottle on top of the piano and hammers out the chords of an immortal tribute to his beloved – thus enabling him to get married and pay off months of overdue rent in the nick of time. This same myth makes it easy to jump to false conclusions about a more business-like approach to songwriting; to assume that, if there is nothing superhuman in the ability to turn out hits, the process is merely mechanical and deplorable. The truth is rather different. Judged as sheet music, the Holland-Dozier-Holland songs do not have the individuality or melodic distinctiveness of, say, Smokey Robinson's. Their virtue lies rather in their conception of lyric, music, group and accompaniment as an integrated structure, in which each has its own distinctive part to play. Thus, in a sense, there can be little 'interpretation' of a Holland-Dozier-Holland song, for it already embodies its own.

What gives these songs their assembly-line quality – I am not using this phrase pejoratively – is their hit-formula repetitiveness. *Baby, I Need Your Loving* gave birth to *Darling, I Hum Our Song*, *Without The One You Love* and *I'll Turn To Stone*, each of which had a similar theme. *Darling, I Hum Our Song* had a title which recalled its predecessor, used a rock 'n' roll triplet backing and was sung in a similar style. *Without The One You Love* actually opened with the words 'Baby I need your good loving'. *I'll Turn To Stone* resembled the model most closely in melodic and harmonic shape but was taken at a different tempo. Similarly *It's The Same Old Song* and *Shake Me, Wake Me* were more melancholy transpositions of *I Can't Help Myself* and *Something About You* respectively. *Reach Out I'll Be There*, their greatest success with The Four Tops, was followed by *Standing In The Shadows Of Love, Bernadette, Seven Rooms Of Gloom* and *You Keep Running Away* (and by *Walk Away Renee* from different hands). Holland, Dozier and Holland know that if a song resembles one that has previously been a hit there is a strong likelihood that it will succeed, so long as the formula is not worked to exhaustion. The song, to return to the terminology of an earlier chapter, is no longer a one-off job but part of a continuing series, and the essential problem, to the solving of which goes considerable time and energy, is one of designing a successful prototype. And that, essentially, is what *Baby, I Need Your Loving* and *Reach Out I'll Be There* were. But this is not to say that song writing becomes uncreative; it is simply that there are limits set upon the creative process. The task of producing variations on a theme is one that can be carried out imaginatively or unimaginatively, according to the abilities of those involved and the pressures under which they work. On the one hand Holland, Dozier and Holland have written songs which effortlessly rework earlier numbers; on the other, in *Reach Out I'll Be There* and its successors they have produced a body of work in which each song has a clearly defined identity and yet there is quite a subtle range of internal references.

That songwriting for a successful group has a logic of its own, which goes beyond the intentions of any one team of songwriters, is evident from the diagram on the page opposite. The Four Tops began their recording career with songs that are relatively simple and cheerful and are concerned with the need for love, but gradually this modulates into a greater concern with isolation and loneliness, the antitheses of love. Perhaps because it is recognised that Levi Stubbs has the ability to tackle stronger and more dramatic material, the songs after *Reach Out I'll Be There*, in which the two

<table>
<tr>
<td rowspan="2">1964–5</td>
<td>

Baby, I Need Your Loving
Darling, I Hum Our Song
Something About You
I Can't Help Myself
</td>
<td rowspan="2">1965–7</td>
<td>

Ask The Lonely
Where Did You Go
Standing In The Shadows of Love
Walk Away Renee
You Keep Running Away
</td>
</tr>
<tr>
<td>

It's The Same Old Song
Without The One You Love
Reach Out I'll Be There
I'll Turn To Stone
</td>
<td>

Reach Out I'll Be There
Seven Rooms of Gloom
Shake Me, Wake Me
Yesterday's Dreams
I'm In A Different World
Lost In A Pool Of Red
</td>
</tr>
</table>

Left lower label: *1965–7*; Right lower label: *1966–9*

LONELINESS   DREAM, ILLUSION

tendencies are held in perfect balance, become more desperate and sombre. With *Yesterday's Dreams* the concern with dream and illusion, already present in *Reach Out, Seven Rooms* and *Shake Me, Wake Me*, becomes more explicit, and the later songs, including *It's All In The Game*, express not anger, resentment or frustration, but a sense of nostalgia and sadness. Thus the records of The Four Tops follow the course of a typical unfulfilled love-affair; the outcome not of self-revelation on the part of Holland, Dozier and Holland or the group, but of the tendency to develop in later songs aspects which were only latent in their predecessors.

Reach Out I'll Be There was a remarkably complex record, which contained so much that it was drawn upon almost inexhaustibly by its successors. According to Brian Holland, it took an hour and three-quarters to make – apparently something of a record by Motown's one-or-two-takes standards. The instrumentation – flutes, oboes, Arab drums – was unusual. The song itself typified Holland, Dozier and Holland's more open approach to song writing. Through extensive use of interludes and transitional sections, their songs invariably have a tripartite construction, the separate sections being linked together very loosely in whatever manner seems most effective for the development of each composition. *Reach Out* and its successors are songs not of a single mood but of conflict, in which the desire for love and happiness struggles against the possibility or reality of loneliness. These emotions are expressed in a complex and relatively consistent musical code. (See table above.) In *Reach Out*, the most optimistic of the five songs, the flute themes predominate, but in *Standing In The Shadows Of Love*, which seems to refer to the earlier song, and

LOVE: HAPPINESS	LONELINESS: SADNESS
chorus	lead
song	speech
flute	guitar: harpsichord
Arabic drums: bongoes	pounding drum
smooth, flowing accompaniment figures	insistent throbbing
even rhythm	changes of tempo: speed-ups and slow-downs
medium tempo	uptempo
clearly defined verse and chorus	monologue – use of motto phrase
sense of aural perspective	absence of aural perspective

envisages future unhappiness, their use has a kind of irony, both mocking and nostalgic. In *Bernadette* they are used only in a very brief section, where the singer speaks of the joy which his heart has always been longing for. The obscurity and perplexity of the singer's feelings in *Bernadette* and *Seven Rooms* is reflected in the disappearance – as it seems to the ordinary listener – of the separation between verse and chorus; the songs assume the character of a dramatic monologue, dominated by the motto phrases of their titles. These songs implicitly refer to *Reach Out I'll Be There* and clearly postulate an acquaintance with that song. *Bernadette* is certainly more powerful in consequence; just as, say, the leitmotivs of *Götterdämmerung* collect resonances from previous operas. This comparison is not to suggest an equivalence between Holland-Dozier-Holland and Wagner – merely that the use of a well-tried formula may have creative potential.

While Holland, Dozier and Holland have undoubtedly made the greatest contribution to the repertoire of The Four Tops, the role of other writers must not be forgotten. *Yesterday's Dreams*, for example, credited to Hunter, Bullock, Goga and Sawyer, is an extremely interesting and very attractive composition. Holland, Dozier and Holland typically alternated unison passages with sections in which the lead was carried over a background of harmonising or antiphonal chanting; in *Yesterday's Dreams*, however, the use of these devices is altogether more complex, the song having an integrated, three-part, circular construction, in which each

The Four Tops. Left to right: Abdul Fakir, Renaldo Benson, Lawrence Payton and Levi Stubbs.

section leads inevitably into the next. The structure is shown in the table below.

I	quiet unison	background harmonising
2	antiphonal chanting	background harmonising
3	antiphonal chanting	full unison

With its effortless succession of diminuendos and crescendos, this seems to be the quintessential pop record of the '60s, transcending the old dichotomy between beat numbers and ballads.

Since *Yesterday's Dreams* and its successors The Four Tops have been lured into the web of transcendental meditation and the vacuous anodynes of abstract 'love' and 'peace'. I cannot say that I am happy about this development, but I am confident that the group can survive it. Superficial 'depth' adds nothing, and detracts but little, from the classic simplicity and strength of the music of The Four Tops.

F

Motown in Review

To turn to some of the rather less celebrated groups and artists who have appeared on Motown labels is to be brought up sharply against the brutal side of merchandising music in mass society, even though most of these artists have probably received a far better deal than they would have had elsewhere. It is not so much that goodwill is lacking, rather that the system imposes necessary restrictions. The problem is one of fierce competition for the record-buyer's limited attention. In the cultural supermarket the objectives are putting one's goods on the shelves, creating in people a predisposition to buy them (by advertising in one form or another), and ensuring that they are prominently displayed and turn over rapidly. Here Motown's brand-name recognisability helps the various acts, because it ensures that their records will receive airplays and be stocked by retailers; because it gives an opportunity for exposure in 'Motortown Revue'; and because the large audience reached by The Supremes and The Four Tops may be favourably disposed towards them too. On the other hand, their goods will be less prominently displayed, they will not be given the best songs to record, and because of an established pecking order they may be placed in the position of a No. 2, not even allowed to try harder. Yet Motown has continued to record a number of acts well after their peak of popularity has been passed. Often, in the time that has elapsed since their first hits, they have noticeably improved. The Marvelettes, for example, on their recent LP 'In Full Bloom', showed themselves to be a far better group than they were when they recorded *When You're Young And In Love*; but how many people care whether or not this is so, care whether the album title is a true statement or mere advertising-man's patter? A novelist can always hope that his neglected work will someday be rediscovered, but there is little prospect of ultimate justice in the world of popular music. Much achievement passes unnoticed, many fine talents are lost without trace once their brief heyday is past. So is it really perverse to insist on the importance of standards in popular music, or to reject the view that all reputations should be subject to the adulation cycle of each generation of fans?

For Motown this is particularly relevant, because in the early days they made a large number of excellent records with girl singers and vocal groups, many of whom have slipped out of sight in the present dominance of popular music by male guitar groups. The first to attract attention was Mary Wells with the light, springy, melodic Smokey Robinson song *My Guy*, very much in the style

Mary Wells, born 13 May 1943.

of Burt Bacharach. Her voice was clear and flexible, yet had an attractive huskiness. Her success encouraged Motown to record similar material with other artists, such as *Looking For The Right Guy* by Kim Weston and *When I'm Gone* by Brenda Holloway. But the superficial charm of this music soon faded, because it depended on obvious devices, like the spreading of a single word over two notes at the end of a line: 'hea-art', sta-art', ca-are'.

Kim Weston married former Motown art director Mickey Stevenson. She left Motown in 1966 to record for MGM.

Left: Chris Clark, perhaps the best white singer Motown has had. She now records for Weed. Right: Brenda Holloway, from Atascadero, California, scored a huge success with Every Little Bit Hurts *(Tamla 54094).*

Fortunately both Kim Weston and Brenda Holloway showed that they were capable of something more substantial. Kim Weston's *Take Me In Your Arms (Rock Me A Little While)* had an intro that was strongly reminiscent of *Where Did Our Love Go?* (for students of the Holland-Dozier-Holland *oeuvre*: it is the link between that song and *You Can't Hurry Love*), but its more relaxed beat and forward-driving tempo made it more like a Stax number, and Kim Weston's fiery preaching of the words was far removed from the coolness of Diana Ross. This splendid record always seems to stand as a reminder of a road that Motown could have taken, but never did. Brenda Holloway was a more convincing singer of the dramatic ballad than Chris Clark, and her version of

Darling Baby (VIP 25029) was the only big hit for The Elgins, who first recorded as The Sensations on Flip in 1958. Right: The Velvelettes' main claim to fame is Needle In A Haystack (VIP 25007), *a success in 1964. They include lead singer Carolyn Gill, Bertha McNeil and Norma Jean Barbee.*

Every Little Bit Hurts showed her at her best. She used the song to express the conflicting emotions of tenderness, pain and anger with great sincerity, and showed how effective melisma could be when used with integrity and restraint. Here we must also mention Hattie Littles' *Your Love Is Wonderful,* a record less overtly emotional than Brenda Holloway's but perhaps more satisfying, because it seemed wholly devoid of contrivance. Hattie Littles sang it with an intense, rapt simplicity which is very difficult to bring off but which on this occasion succeeded. These three performances are classics of the early Motown period.

If typecasting has been a problem even for some of the leading Motown groups, it is hardly surprising that it should have affected others even more seriously. The Elgins have specialised in ingratiating, slow-to-medium-tempo ballads like *Darlin' Baby, Put Yourself In My Place* and *It's Been A Long, Long Time,* which became excessively mannered. The Velvelettes had two hits with

86

the similar *Needle In The Haystack* and *Bird In The Hand,* in which proverbial wisdom was endowed with a certain jauntiness, though the hand-clapping on the former sounded more like a jackbooted march-past of the *Wehrmacht.* But The Marvelettes' *Please Mr. Postman* and *Beechwood 4-5789* had a gaiety and a lively swing (for which the rhythm section must take most of the credit) which put them among the very best of Motown's High School recordings. In recent years the group has moved from songs of innocence to songs of experience. If the melodies still tend to be syrupy (*Seeing Is Believing, That's How Heartaches Are Made*) the singing itself is soulful. The new lead, Ann Bogan, who replaced Gladys Horton when she left the group in 1968, showed that on numbers like *The Truth's Outside My Door* and *At Last I See Love As It Really Is* she was capable of singing with a raw-voiced, bitter knowingness which quite exposed the sighing background harmonies. Probably the old and by now inappropriate image of The Marvelettes was holding them back from stronger things.

Less fortunate in their progress were The Contours, who suffered a series of damaging personnel changes and, when they folded in 1968, had become little more than a second-string Four Tops. But their early discs had a brash irreverence, an exploding energy that typified Motown at its exciting early best, a sound that

The Marvelettes were originally five girls from Inkster High—Gladys Horton, Wanda Rogers, Katherine Anderson, Georgianna Tillman and Juanita Cowan. Now a trio, Horton, Rogers and Anne Bogan are the present singers. Right: The Contours were introduced to Berry Gordy Jr by Jackie Wilson. They had a million-seller in Do You Love Me *(Gordy 7005), and their personnel has included Hugh Davis, Silvester Potts, Conrad Guy, Hubert Johnson, Joe Billingsea, Bill Hoggs, Billy Gordon, Joe Stubbs, Gerald Green and Dennis Edwards.*

was easily imitated but never equalled. Records of this period were often deliberately camp, as in The Contours' *First I Look At The Purse*, with its coy 'What does every man look at first?', and The

Monitors' *Greetings This Is Uncle Sam* – though time has turned the opening lines of the latter,

> I want to take you to a far off land,
> to lend a helping hand,
> I need you,

into a very sick joke indeed. The frenetic energy of The Isley Brothers closely linked them with The Contours in the revival of rock music in the early '60s, and it was natural that they should for a time be associated with Motown, for whom they cut two of their highest voltage sides, *This Old Heart Of Mine* and *Behind A Painted Smile*. Their skill lay in setting an easy, rocking groove while at the same time sustaining a level of theatrical intensity from the first note to the last. By comparison more recent groups have sounded relatively tame. The Fantastic Four scarcely lived up to their name,

The Jackson Five once recorded for Steel Town, a label in Gary, Indiana. Their first four Motown singles have sold over ten million copies. Right: Junior Walker: his first big hit was Shotgun.

while The Originals, although certainly original in their use of complex close harmonies, were in danger, with *Green Grow The Lilacs*, of sounding merely pretty and they did not appear to have yet developed a consistent style. Under Marvin Gaye's guidance they seemed to grasp the importance of a strong lead, and *Baby I'm For Real* was altogether more promising. But the most promising of the new Motown groups was The Jackson Five. Though there was obviously a danger that they might be exploited, like Stevie Wonder, in a gimmicky way – as with *A.B.C.* – *I Want You Back* was a tremendously exciting first disc, obviously highly disciplined in the relationship between voices and rhythmic accompaniment and yet with a feeling of spontaneity. Michael Jackson's vocal delivery suggested the possibility of restoring an openness to Motown's more, supple, but still inflexible, bongo-based style through the use of rock 'n' roll breaks.

Motown's discotheque sounds are provided by the supercharged, larger-than-life interpretations of Junior Walker and Bobby Taylor – enjoyable music of its kind and no more disposable than

most. Junior Walker's version of *How Sweet It Is (To Be Loved By You)* may not be as good as Marvin Gaye's but it is rhythmically irresistible, and anyone required to choose between the two would find the decision impossible and insist on keeping both.

Motown has signed a number of good male singers, but they do not seem to have been able to do themselves justice, either because of the lack of suitable material, or because the Motown emphasis on groups has made them take a back seat. David Ruffin is still the best of them, but since I have already written about him in the chapter on The Temptations there is little to add here, except that, without

Edwin Starr performing his **Agent 00 Soul** *routine. Right: Chuck Jackson, once of the Del-Vikings: he previously recorded for Wand.*

a regular group to show-case his style, his vocal lines tend to sound rather stilted, and he has still to find a format in which he can give of his best. Jimmy Ruffin, his brother, has had a number of ballad hits, which unfortunately represent the nadir of the Motown formula. The refrain is battered out, with male voice choir accompaniment, in a manner painfully reminiscent of an old Hollywood soundtrack. The effect is like beginning every word with a capital letter. For example, in *What Becomes Of The Brokenhearted* we find 'I can't stand this *Pain Much Longer*' and 'All that's left is an

Unhappy Ending'. This profitable formula has straitjacketed Jimmy Ruffin's abilities as an artist. Marv Johnson's *I'll Pick A Rose For My Rose* is in a similar vein.

Chuck Jackson is a somewhat improved singer, who now has a more soulful, less Capitol-Records sort of sound, but as yet this consists largely of empty mannerisms, delivered with a good deal of energy but without much conviction. Edwin Starr proved himself, on the Golden World label, to be a singer of great promise, able to bridge the baritone and tenor registers, having a way with both ballads and uptempo numbers and a good-natured ebullience that was strongly reminiscent of the young Marvin Gaye, to whom he appeared a potential successor. His records with Motown, however, have so far been disappointing; there is a great deal of smoke but the

Frederick 'Shorty' Long had the first release on the Motown Soul subsidiary in April 1964 – Devil With The Blue Dress (35001). From Alabama, he was, with Amos Milburn and Eddie Burns, one of the company's bluesiest performers. He died in a boating accident in June 1969.

fire seems temporarily to have gone out. But that there are still grounds for hope would seem to be confirmed by the work of Shorty Long, who made a number of good discotheque records like *Function At The Junction, Devil With A Blue Dress* and *Here Comes The Judge*, but in 'The Prime of Shorty Long', an album made shortly before he died at the age of twenty-nine, revealed a hitherto unsuspected range and interpretative skill. Shorty Long was typical of the new generation of bluesmen in the way in which he united church and secular traditions – a synthesis not achieved easily but only through continual application. Ragni L. Griffin has described how 'the churchy timbre of his voice became bluesy from listening for hours to records by Johnny Ace and Little Willie John'.

That Shorty Long was 'ready' at the time of his death is abundantly evident from 'The Prime of Shorty Long'; there is a mellowness, a mature self-confidence, which comes from the knowledge that the severest challenges have been set and overcome. On almost every track Shorty Long attempts the impossible. There are soulful versions of *Memories Are Made Of This* and *When You Are Available*, and highly individual interpretations of Fats Domino numbers like *I'm Walkin'* and *Blue Monday*, which had seemed untouchable. But the most remarkable tracks are *A Whiter Shade Of Pale* and his own composition *I Had A Dream*, which have a sombre, apocalyptic intensity, a brooding, trance-like solemnity that is positively disturbing. In both, death seems to be present, and the annihilation of the pain of existence is seen as something at once frightening and ecstatic.

Stevie Wonder is an artist who has not yet reached maturity but has nevertheless made great progress since he became famous at the age of thirteen with his recording of *Fingertips*. *Fingertips* was little more than recorded hysteria, but it did show that even then Stevie Wonder had a special magnetism, which enabled him to communicate strongly and to compel an audience to become involved in what he was doing. He is at his best when he is not actually singing, in the conventional sense. It is, in fact, the weak point of his ballads and more commercial records that he does sing on them. Stevie Wonder has been strongly influenced by Ray Charles, but his present style is his own, because, whereas Ray Charles tends to create large spaces in his music, Stevie Wonder builds a dramatic performance by eliminating them, desperately pressing words upon each other, slipping and sliding back and forward between chanting, shouting and crying. He has made five outstanding records, *Uptight, I Was Made To Love Her, Shoo-Be-Doo-Be-Doo-Da-Day, For Once In My Life* and *Signed, Sealed, Delivered*, but the best of them by far is *I Was Made To Love Her*. His ability to shift accents continually while maintaining the integrity of the vocal line gives his singing a built-in syncopation; by phrasing slightly off the beat and then catching up with it at emphatic moments he is able to create a pattern of stresses that is both varied and naturally climactic. *I Was Made To Love Her* sets a standard that it will be hard to live up to.

In the case of Marvin Gaye and Gladys Knight, who must be regarded as the most substantial artists on the Motown label apart from the well-established original groups, any attempt to talk about

When Fingertips *(Tamla 54080) sold a million copies Stephen Judkins was dubbed 'The Twelve Year Old Genius'. Now, as Stevie Wonder, he is perhaps the company's most talented performer. Right: Gladys Knight and The Pips, Merald Knight, William Guest and Edward Patton, recorded for Fury and Maxx before joining Motown.*

them purely in terms of musical achievement would limit the scope of inquiry too narrowly. Again, the abstraction of the Tin Pan Alley 'standard' constitutes a limiting perspective. A blues invariably starts from a concrete situation, even if a common one, but the 'standard' merely supplies generalised words about 'love', envisaged as a subject for discussion. It is always 'about' something, yet invariably lacks a clearly defined subject. In black music, on the other hand, every song is a miniature drama and the singer is an actor who plays a distinctive part. So, in considering Marvin Gaye and Gladys Knight, we are concerned not only with their qualities as singers but with their ability to get inside a part, to perform an assigned role. But this role is also one that types them, that defines,

Tammi Terrell made eleven singles and three albums with Marvin Gaye.

to some extent, their public image; which means that in practice they cannot sing any song but one consonant with their role. This

98

in turn relates to a typology, in part mythical, in part related to experience, within the black community. Men and women are seen as being of two kinds, one predatory, ruthless and sexually magnetic, the other tender, faithful and vulnerable. This distinction carries with it no moral overtones; it is simply a law of kinds. What made Otto Preminger's adaptation of Bizet in *Carmen Jones* so effective was that it fitted pre-existing stereotypes; and Harry Belafonte's tragedy in part consisted of the fact that he mistook his own nature. Among singers, James Brown (with songs like *It's A Man's World*) and Diana Ross can be regarded as representatives of the first type, David Ruffin and Gladys Knight of the second. But virtually all songs stress the likelihood of an unstable and ultimately temporary relationship, for even the happy and joyful ones, like Marvin Gaye and Tammi Terrell's *Good Lovin' Ain't Easy To Come By*, suggest that this is the exception to a general rule. Because relationships have for a variety of reasons, assumed a less institutionalised form within the black community, love assumes a great deal more

99

Marvin Gaye, Tamla's most successful male soloist, sang with popular mid-'50s groups including The Moonglows and The Rainbows. He comes from Washington, D.C., and plays piano, drums and guitar. Right: Tammi Terrell, originally Tammi Montgomery, died from a brain tumour on 16 March 1970.

importance, for a woman has to hold on to her man, and a man to his woman, without relying on the bourgeois legal sanctions of the marriage ceremony. It is the man's prerogative to leave when he wishes; it is his right if he finds that his woman has been unfaithful. The songs of Gladys Knight reflect this greater freedom that is

ascribed to the man, for another woman, a sexual rival, invariably figures prominently in them. Songs like *Don't Let Her Take Your Love From Me* and *(I Know) I'm Losing You* express anxiety at the breaking-up of a relationship, while *The End Of Our Road* and *Don't Turn Me Away* deal with the moment of parting. *Just Walk In My Shoes* and *Didn't You Know (You'd Have To Cry Sometime)* express a desire that the man also shall learn to suffer the pain of rejection; while both *It Should Have Been Me* and *All I Could Do Is Cry* portray the feelings of a woman who witnesses the marriage of her man to somebody else. Similarly *I Know Better* suggests that sexual surrender may lead to future regret. These situations and roles are obviously conventional, but they nevertheless enable a singer like Gladys Knight to draw on a range of feeling far beyond the compass of an ordinary 'standard', and to speak in a way that is both immediate and dramatic.

The role assumed by Marvin Gaye is more complex, for he does not appear simply as the tender and faithful lover. In his songs Gaye appears as an ideal synthesis of opposites. On the one hand he is strongly independent and insists on retaining his self-respect. If a woman is unfaithful he will leave her – *I'll Be Doggone, I Got To Get To California, So Long*. This only makes him seem more of a man, for his independence is exerted in a just cause. On the other hand, there are songs in which he is tender and romantic; and his work with Tammi Terrell conveys a vision of mutual harmony and trust. In fact this partnership, now ended as a result of Tammi Terrell's early death, was a kind of symbolic marriage – expressed pictorially on the album cover on which they appeared together, within the enlarged 'U' of 'United.' The success of their records can be attributed to the fact that the rapport they achieve was not merely musical but seemed to express a genuine warmth and affection. As on the stage, the art lay in playing a role with such fidelity that it did not appear to be one.

In recent years, Marvin Gaye and Gladys Knight appear to have been engaged in a private cutting contest with a number of Whitfield-Strong compositions, like *That's The Way Love Is, I Heard It Through The Grapevine, The End Of Our Road* and *Don't You Miss Me A Little Bit Baby* – songs which are a good deal more interesting than the writers' work for The Temptations. Comparing the versions reveals their individual strengths. Marvin Gaye is the more self-conscious interpreter; in every song the phrasing, from beginning to end, appears to have been carefully pondered, and he has an astonishing vocal range and control over timbre and voice production. Listen, for example, to *Yesterday*, where he makes use of a freakishly high, open tenor register yet retains the rough cutting edge of his voice. Gaye's versions of *That's The Way Love Is* and *I Heard It Through The Grapevine* are subtly shaded, carefully articulated dramatic structures, which make skilful use of diminuendo and crescendo and seem to have been designed for records. Those of Gladys Knight and The Pips, however, have a hard-driving immediacy, which makes them more like in-person performances. Gladys Knight has the rare ability to give melodic freshness even to the most uninteresting song, by slightly altering the contours of the vocal line. The Pips, the male voice trio which supports her, contribute equally vitally to the group's success. Together Gladys Knight and The Pips always swing strongly, because they have retained the energy of the classic call-and-response patterns of gospel music at something very close to their best. Although it is impossible not to admire the artistry of Marvin Gaye, who on his recent records has shown an interpretative technique and sensitivity virtually unequalled in popular music, I still prefer the work of Gladys Knight, because she seems more personally involved in what she is singing, and because there is never any risk that she will lose sight of the realities to which the words refer. If proof is needed of the strength of the contemporary synthesis of gospel and the blues, there is no need to look further than Gladys Knight and The Pips.

Music, Black and White

We were very heavily influenced by blues and rock 'n' roll at first. Then we got into more of a pop approach; then we got into straight blues, and then country. We've really played a bit of everything.
Mick Jagger

I wanted to express more anger and emotion in sound, and the obvious step towards further expression was to get a Moog.
Keith Emerson

There is an excitement about their presence and careful management has ensured that just the right amount of Led Zeppelin is fed to the hungry fans. They do not release singles. They are never seen in British TV.
Melody Maker

The above quotations indicate, in shorthand form, some of the pressures operating in contemporary popular music, pressures which affect Motown artists as much as anybody else. The aim of this final chapter is to consolidate a number of points which have been touched on in earlier chapters, and at the same time to raise some larger issues – for I confess that my interest in Motown is not solely in the music but also in the light it sheds on the way in which existing institutions can assimilate and modify forces which make, however feebly or unselfconsciously, for cultural change. It must not be forgotten that the role assigned to popular music has been that of a safety valve for feelings which could not find expression elsewhere. Rock 'n' roll was a vehicle for inarticulate rebellion at the height of the cold war, and later in the '60s popular music helped to focus the resistance of the young to American imperialism in south-east Asia. Yet even here we find a process of containment at work. If black music was the foundation

Over page: The Supremes and The Temptations in the NBC television show 'Taking Care of Business', shown on 9 December 1968.

on which rock 'n' roll was built, the '60s, despite Motown, saw no real expansion of the area of black music.

To discover why, we must repeat the question: why was Motown so successful? Some answers have already been given, but one which is as important as any is that the large record companies were not recording, and were not interested in recording, black music. If we ask further, why, if Motown was so successful, it and Stax did not represent the dominant trend in the '60s, then our answer must in part be the same. Motown came in on the heels of Spector and British pop, but it was up against very strong institutional forces – the large record companies, who define at any time what popular music 'is'.

In this context American Columbia (CBS) offers a significant example. Columbia, because of its size, power, distribution system and affiliations with the CBS radio and television network, can legitimately be regarded as a representative large record company. There is, of course, nothing sinister about Columbia; it shows a good deal of discrimination in signing artists and gives them a great deal of latitude and support. But anything Columbia decides to do necessarily has consequences because of its size and influence.

In recent years the company has been badly caught out on more than one occasion. Rock 'n' roll was an unexpected body blow to its pre-eminence in the popular music of the Mitch Miller era. It did little better in the High School period, was taken unprepared by the upsurge of interest in the Liverpool sound and British rock, and was largely left out, or preferred to stay out, of the 'soul explosion'. Yet at present Columbia is close to recapturing its former eminence, having involved itself successively in country, folk, jazz-rock and progressive music. Considered purely as a study in company rivalry – which is certainly a relevant perspective, if not the only one – the history of popular music can be seen as a series of successive and ultimately unsuccessful challenges to Columbia's brand leadership, by RCA (Elvis and C & W), Capitol (British pop) and relatively small independents like Motown and Atlantic-Stax (soul). If they failed, if the crazes petered out, one of the many reasons is the fact that Columbia had no interest in their continuance. Anything in which Columbia was not involved must, by definition, be a minor trend.

When Columbia has recorded black artists it has done so because they could be presented either as tasteful (Johnny Mathis) or as geniuses (Thelonius Monk) or both (Miles Davis). Columbia had Miles Davis much as *The New Yorker* had James Baldwin. The company must be regarded as the true progenitor of contemporary hype, because it always insinuates that everyone who records for it must be a genius or something approaching one, and because it clearly prefers artists who can be passed off as such, from Dave Brubeck to such contemporary figures as Simon and Garfunkel, Leonard Cohen, Moby Grape and Blood, Sweat and Tears. Artists as diverse as Leonard Bernstein, Barbra Streisand and Bob Dylan are linked not so much by talent (for others have that too) as by the indefinable, CBS-trademarked aura of power, mystery and devastating sophistication. CBS artists are given expensive and deferential receptions, and receive favourable exposure in the media. (Brubeck and Monk appeared on the cover of *Time*. 'Why *Brubeck*?' people muttered at the time; and, in a different tone, 'Why *Monk*?'.) The prestige of some rubs off on others; the *Record Mirror* (26 September 1970) observed:

At the New York rock-palace, such luminaries as Miles Davis and Leonard Bernstein have been noted in the audience when BS & T has played there.

– 'luminaries', of course, being a very CBS word.

Columbia hype works because it recognises the adman's old dictum that there must always be a tiny core of truth in any claim. (As in the case of the beer bottles that were washed in 'Live Steam'.) It is successful because it is seldom found out (unlike The Monkees) and because it works as well with the underground as with the establishment, with *Rolling Stone* as much as *Time*. Columbia's white orientation is one important reason why black music, successful as it is, still remains in a cultural ghetto.

Black music is confronted with a situation in which it can never win, even with Motown or Invictus. It could not even have succeeded with the black music company which Otis Redding wanted to found. The emphasis on white music promulgated by the large record companies reinforces a corresponding bias in white youth culture, which in turn is supported by the prejudices of the progressive music press and the preferences of TV programmers. Black music itself is distorted because it is valued in so far as it reflects white music and has affiliations with it. If, for example, people are disposed to take Sly and The Family Stone seriously, it is largely because they are, unlike most black groups, a 'band'; because they are racially integrated; and because they work in the white progressive idiom. This is not to deny white music's right to develop in its own way, but to point to the casualties which it leaves in its triumphant wake. The growth of hard rock has wiped out large areas of modern jazz and with it a tiny and hard-won field of employment open only to the outstanding black musicians. (Not always to all of those. In the heyday of progressive and West Coast jazz, musicians of the calibre of J. J. Johnson worked on the assembly line.) In the new structure that white culture is building black music has little place. Atlantic Records, having made a fortune out of black artists, are now promoting, and building a mystique around, white groups like Crosby, Stills, Nash and Young and Led Zeppelin. In the values of the underground press 'white' black music such as Motown's is reviled, but white 'black' music is continually praised and discussed and receives infinitely more attention than the music it imitates. It is all rather reminiscent of the progressive jazz era, when aficionados who knew the name of every Kenton sideman past and present had never even heard of Clifford Brown, Fats Navarro or Bud Powell. Black musicians are now implicitly regarded as precursors who, having taught the white man all they know, must gradually recede into the distance, as white progressive music, the simple lessons mastered, advances irresistibly into the future.

The processes at work here can be paralleled elsewhere in contemporary society. The main concepts required are those of 'negative definition' and 'positive reinforcement'; together they make up a 'mental set' that both defines and to some extent constitutes reality. Negative definition may be compared to the focusing mechanism of a reflex camera, which, at a sufficiently large aperture, excludes what is not required for the picture from its field of vision. Positive reinforcement can be likened to a rangefinder camera in which things become clear and in focus only when one image is superimposed upon another. Thus, in a musical context, popular music is negatively defined by what the companies decide to put on disc – this, for all practical purposes, is what popular music 'is'. Similarly the news is what appears in the newspapers and on television and what does not appear there is *ipso facto* not news. Positive reinforcement is slightly more complex. This implies that little is to be gained if record companies or news media send out conflicting messages, since this only undermines their own credibility. All will have more influence if they all say the same thing or converge on the same objective. Their joint concern with a certain subject establishes that subject as real, much as a vision is validated by the evidence of several eye-witnesses. It does not really matter if this consensus, so arrived at, is genuinely representative of popular opinion (value), or if it is a truthful representation of reality (fact), since it predicates its own representativeness and defines its own reality; what does matter is that the record companies or news media shall largely agree among themselves.

That this situation has been imperfectly recognised can chiefly be attributed to the work of Marshall McLuhan, who has discoursed on the intrinsic properties of television like a medieval alchemist on the Philosopher's Stone. McLuhan is blind to the fact that media can be used in different ways both by those who control them and by those who are exposed to them. Fidel Castro's television speeches, for example, represent a use of the medium which, according to McLuhan, is impossible. Moreover, he thus distracts attention both from the specific uses of the media for social control and, in his apocalyptic emphasis on the supplanting of print culture by the electronic village, from the role television plays within a total media context. But he is incorrect even in the qualities he attributes to television, for he has spoken of its appeal to the young in terms of total involvement – and the very reason for young people's disinterest in television is that it does not involve. A rock concert fails on television, because its volume is radically diminished and the constant cutting, necessitated by television's low-definition image, pushes the viewer away. A movie on television fails in the same manner, because its images do not carry the weight, on a small screen and in a conversation-filled, illuminated living room, which they have in a quiet, darkened cinema.

In a total media context the role of television is precisely that of positive reinforcement. Television cannot conflict with the press because this would give it the appearance of being partisan and undermine its claim to authoritativeness; it cannot take sides because of its obligation to be impartial and because its dependence on the government makes it vulnerable. All television can do is serve as a gigantic reflector, sending back what it receives from the capitalist press, one thousand times magnified. Television is the *status quo* in CinemaScope. The relationship between media and government recalls the medieval rapport of Church and State, while control of the media is analogous to the monopoly of the printed word enjoyed by the priestly class. The convergence of the media, the establishment of a consensus is dictated by the ideological need to provide a common mental set and to confirm an image of reality as reality itself. The question, of course, is whether there is anybody listening. Although media are often facilely spoken of in terms of communication, the communication is all one way and, as technology multiplies the means of disseminating information, it also gradually eliminates feed back.

The media's own definition of themselves in terms of 'rationality' and an 'objective world', their tendency to converge, is both counterpointed and complemented by the underground's definition of itself as subjective and irrational, as a divergent world in which everyone thinks as he likes. Thus the impossibility, among other things, of a 'criticism' of pop music. For the prophet of the underground there is only 'myself', 'what is relevant to me'; for the mass media an abstract 'general will' that negates the authenticity of any individual or group. Dialectical interplay between argument and argument, thought and action, group and group is effectively ruled out. Both official culture and counter-culture are characterised by their selective attention ('All the news that fits'), by their refusal to acknowledge the existence of what they do not wish to see, a refusal that is ultimately paranoid.

How natural, therefore, that the youth culture of popular music and the mass society of the mass media should choose to remain encapsulated within their own separate worlds.

Tamla Motown
TRADE MARK OF MOTOWN RECORD CORPORATION